Parables
OF
Hope

Foreword by Joni Eareckson Tada

Parables
OF
Hope

Inspiring Truths from
People with Disabilities

Allen Jay Hoogewind

ZondervanPublishingHouse
Grand Rapids, Michigan

A Division of HarperCollinsPublishers

Parables of Hope
Copyright © 1998 by Allen Jay Hoogewind

Requests for information should be addressed to:

ZondervanPublishingHouse
Grand Rapids, Michigan 49530

Library of Congress Cataloging-in-Publication Data

Hoogewind, Allen Jay, 1942–.
   Parables of hope : Inspiring truths from people with disabilities / Allen Jay
Hoogewind.
      p. cm.
   ISBN 0-310-21624-9 (softcover)
    1. Church work with the handicapped—Case studies. 2. Handicapped—
Religious life—Case studies. I. Title.
BV4460.H66 1998
259'.4—dc21   97-35475
      CIP

Interior design by Jody DeNeef

Printed in the United States of America

98 99 00 01 02 03 04 /❖ DC/ 10 9 8 7 6 5 4 3 2 1

I want to thank my wife, Coral, for listening to me tell the stories of Christian friends who have disabilities. Her encouragement and support for the venture of putting these stories into print was the push I needed to make this effort become a reality.

But I want to dedicate this book to the many individuals with disabilities who have been an inspiration to me. Their spontaneous expressions of agape love and their simple but solid faith have been a valuable ministry to me even as I have been called upon to minister to them. To the Erics, Catherines, Sallys, Johns, Judys, Steves, Melanies, and the many other people who have shared their lives with me as I have experienced parables of hope, I dedicate this book.

Contents

it is necessary to have the gift of sight to serve the Lord. His life and his words raise the question, What is "normal" anyway?

Judy appears before her church board to profess her faith in Jesus Christ. The elders and deacons wonder if she understands the significance of her faith as a person with mental retardation, cerebral palsy, and a mobility impairment. But she disarms them with her profound understanding of the church in the breaking of the bread and drinking from the cup.

The testimony of God's working in the life of Steve was never so powerfully expressed as at his funeral. He became a paraplegic because of a diving accident. His disability provided many opportunities for God to use him to touch the lives of others. Some of these people spoke of this at his funeral.

Dick is mildly retarded. He works in the warehouse of Zondervan Publishing House. He unashamedly and spontaneously shares the joy of his faith with everyone he meets.

Melanie has severe learning difficulties. She is able to worship meaningfully with the rest of her fellow church members by watching closely and imitating the worship style of those around her.

Gary, a recent college graduate, has communicated by reading the lips of his family, friends, professors, and fellow students and by signing. Upon graduation he learns that an operation could give him up to 100 percent hearing. What does he decide?

Dennis has the rare Prader-Willi syndrome disability. Almost everything he eats turns to pounds. His experience of God's grace doesn't take his craving for food away but is absolutely essential to addressing it.

The Pine Rest Chapel service is truly worship for and by persons with differing mental impairments. Prayers are offered by the congregation. Special music is provided by those whose gifts may not be appreciated by most church people because of the lack of professionalism. But their worship is truly "in spirit and in truth."

Chris is a gifted woman; gifted in the truest sense of the gifts of the Holy Spirit. She can't talk, and she doesn't write stories. She doesn't walk, and she doesn't have full control of her arm movements. But she can paint! God's grace oozes out a tube of paint and onto a canvas.

Frances has had schizophrenia more than forty years. Her friends are dying all around her, and she knows that she will die soon. She doesn't see her family much anymore, but she wants a funeral that will let her family know where she stands with her God.

Fourteen years ago Robert had a major car accident and was left with a severe traumatic head injury and other major disabling conditions, including alcoholism. His life has been a roller-coaster series of one complication after another. His faith in Jesus Christ today is deeper and more sincere than it has ever been in his life.

Harold has limited use of one arm and walks with a pronounced limp. He seems to give the impression that he doesn't need others in his life, but beneath his harsh tones we sense that he needs and craves encouragement from those who really make a difference in his life.

Penny speaks for many of her friends when she is asked to describe God's grace in a Bible study at her church youth group. Her words give a message congruent to the actions that flow from her daily life. God graciously loves people through the unconditional, spontaneous love of his people who have disabilities.

Foreword

Before you begin . . .

I've gotten used to being on display. Whether it's the child studying my wheelchair, the senior citizen across the way smiling sympathetically, or the waiter eyeing me carefully as I use my bent spoon to eat pieces of hamburger, I am aware that people are watching. Some might watch out of pity, some out of admiration. All watch, I sense, with unspoken questions.

Allen Hoogewind has tenderly and effectively put his disabled friends on display to answer questions all of us have about life, ourselves, and God. Each *Parable* in this gallery gives a glimpse of God's enduring hope in the midst of pain. Fred's irrepressible need to be a part of church, Colleen's daily birthday party, and Judy's quest to take Communion are powerful lessons of what it means to be alive and to hope.

But Allen's friends are more than audiovisual aids of hope. Allen is not content to make us simply feel better about ourselves by learning of someone else's joys and struggles. He seeks more than an inspired readership. He seeks our betterment by engaging us to move into relationship with people with disabilities. Although his friends and I are privileged to be on display for God's glory, we find much greater joy in being treated as citizens of equal standing in Christ's kingdom. And that is why I am particularly grateful for Allen's ministry and his book. *Parables of Hope* is more than a book about unique individuals.

It is about the hope that he and I share: Christ's church will someday embrace all of its members.

Our hope is founded on three truths regarding people with disabilities and our relationship with them. First, they are people with souls who have been included in God's *redemptive plan*. They are more than fabricated, one-dimensional parables. They are people for whom Christ died and for whom the message of Christ's hope is painfully real. And once redeemed, their souls yearn with great intensity for heavenly redemption. You can feel the intensity of their soul's desire for heaven as you read *Parables of Hope*. Check your pulse if you don't!

Disabled people are not only a part of God's redemptive plan, but also a part of God's *corporate design*. A redeemed person with a disability is an intricate part of what Christ commanded about his church. As Chuck Swindoll told his congregation one day concerning those who are disabled, "They are not in our way, they are a part of our way." People with disabilities can serve, usher, teach, lead, help, comfort—each according to his or her giftedness and all according to God's grace. Answer Allen's questions at the end of each parable and you will not be able to deny the blessed tie that binds us together.

The redemptive and inclusive hope to which Allen and I cling is not to be kept secret from the world. God designed our relationship to be a *cultural witness*. When the thirty-five-year-old man with Down's syndrome is welcomed in a small country church in South Dakota, it speaks volumes to his relatives, his social worker, and his employer at Pizza Hut. They see not only that Christ's commands are taken seriously, but also that the church is a place where they, in their own hurts and weaknesses, might find comfort and strength. A church that loves a person with a disability trumpets God's love to a loveless and hopeless world.

Parables, as well as Allen's ministry at Hope Network, exemplifies the hope of Christ for each of us and his church. What a wonderful thing it would be if one of these parables could be read each week in church! Jesus would be proud if we listened carefully. He would be prouder still if we obeyed and embraced his living parables among us.

Joni Eareckson Tada
JAF Ministries

Preface

Christians who are disabled have many things in common with other people of the church. But nothing is so basic as being another human being created in the image of God. Having a disability makes a person no more saintly—or less saintly—than a T.A.B. (temporarily able-bodied) brother or sister in Christ. Individuals with disabilities put their clothes on in the morning, love the smell of lilacs on a new spring morning, get discouraged and angry when others shun them, and face the challenges of life much as do pastors, church leaders, and all other members of the church.

Therefore persons with disabilities, like all the rest of God's people, have a place in the church and can make a contribution to the ministry that all God's people share in. They have stories to tell—parables of God's grace. Stories that are often profound in their simplicity and straightforward honesty. Stories that all too often God's people do not hear. And stories that remind us of the parables of Jesus in that they are lessons in God's grace in the context of his kingdom.

Many people in the church are uncomfortable with brothers and sisters in Christ who look or talk differently because of their disabilities. Such church people avoid making meaningful contact with this part of the church, and therefore they fail to hear the stories of grace that people with disabilities have to tell. Maybe many people in the church do not think that God's people with disabilities have much to tell. I suspect that many of those with disabilities themselves do not believe they have much worthwhile to contribute to the rest of God's people. For various reasons they are often not given the opportunity to give their testimony to the grace of God. I strongly believe that persons with disabilities need to tell their stories and I believe that God's people need to hear how God works in their lives. For it is when all of God's people share their gifts that all of God's people are blessed.

I have the unique privilege of serving as a chaplain at Hope Network in Grand Rapids, Michigan. Hope Network is a large Christian organization in which people are committed to assist men and women with disabilities to develop all aspects of their lives. Chaplains work alongside residential staff, work trainers, social workers, occupational therapists, speech therapists, transportation drivers, and a large support staff of secretaries, business-office people, and management people. Our mission is to "enhance the dignity and independence of people who are disabled and disadvantaged." By the empowerment of God's grace, together we seek to live, work, and worship God to the fullest extent of our abilities. Our focus is more on people's abilities (and gifts) than on their disabilities. With varying degrees of effectiveness we attempt to avoid a "them-us" mentality. We have much to learn from each other.

Hope Network ministers to more than five thousand people with disabilities who live, work, and receive treatment in many locations around Michigan. Some of their residences are group homes that have as few as five people, while others live in a forty-bed old nurses' dormitory. Some people require almost total care, others need assistance of professionals. Some of my friends with disabilities work in sheltered workshops, where they have jobs geared to their abilities, while others work throughout the community. My ministry takes me to this wide range of circumstances.

The stories I write in this book are parables of real people and real events in their lives. In most cases I have changed their names and enough of their circumstances to protect their anonymity. However, I have used the real names and circumstances of four people in this book because their lives have been more public and many people will recognize them. With either their permission or that of a family member, their names are Eric Davis (chapter 9), Rev. Jim Vanderlaan (chapter 12), Steve Johnson (chapter 14), and Chris Lake (chapter 20).

I felt a strong calling from God to write this book and in this way assist my Christian friends to share stories of God's grace with you. *Parables of Hope* is intended to affirm individuals with disabilities as God's people who are valuable and important to your and my life as children of God's kingdom. We, the church, need to learn from all members of Christ's body. The Bible invites and challenges us to be open to each other's gifts. I trust that you will find the stories inspirational and insightful, much like the parables Jesus told his disciples. If there is a central theme in the many truths that I have learned from individuals with disabilities, it is that God's grace is experienced in the midst of pain, struggle, and heartache. The joy, peace, patience, perseverance, and love that so many of my friends experience are against the backdrop of unique challenges and weaknesses in life. It is my prayer that you will continue to be blessed by God's grace that flows from your friends and your fellow church members with disabilities.

"I'm here too, so please notice me."

> *Now you are the body of Christ, and each one of*
> *you is a part of it.*
>
> 1 Corinthians 12:27

Life is sometimes a bit hectic in an adult-care foster home, especially when there are twelve people who have to be bathed, eat breakfast, and find the appropriate Sunday clothes for worship—and when all this has to be done before the 9:30 A.M. church worship service. But Fred has gone through this routine many times before: Get up at 6:00 in the morning, be the second in line to use the shower, receive minimal but basic assistance with his bathing, brushing teeth, and combing hair routine. Fred can do most of this himself, but his personal care attendant, Dennis, makes sure Fred doesn't miss anything, especially the underarm deodorant, which he frequently forgets.

Then he has to be sitting down by 6:40 A.M. to eat along with the others in the second-shift breakfast. By 7:10 Fred uses his walker to go to the laundry room to get his nice green-striped shirt and black trousers, which by now he has identified as his "go-to-church clothes." He returns to his room. Listens to hymns on the radio. Gets dressed for church. (Fred is especially proud that he can now button his shirt. He did not have the hand dexterity to do that six months ago, but he worked on this skill in his day classes at the day center.) He comes out of the bedroom to ask his personal care attendant if he looks good enough to go to church. This is all part of the routine that is all too familiar in Fred's group home.

If Fred were paying attention to what was happening out-side his shower room, kitchen, and bedroom throughout the morning, he would see all his friends scurrying around getting ready for church just as he is doing. He would notice the three staff persons on duty that day who are attending to the person-al needs of Fred's eleven housemates. The goal of these staff members is to teach each person to assume as much personal responsibility for himself or herself as that person is able to handle. "Got to be responsible for myself" is the message that each person in the twelve-bed adult foster care home frequent-ly says to himself or herself.

Fred loves to go to church. He is happy that at this group home there are Christians on staff who go out of their way to make sure that he and his roommates who want to attend church will have the opportunity to go. Fred knows only too well that he has not always been allowed to go to church, even though his parents and he had wanted this to happen since the first time he left home and entered his first adult foster care home eighteen years ago. He was thirty-nine years old when his mother died. Because his dad could not take care of him any-more, he decided to send Fred to that first A.F.C. home by the bridge across town.

When his dad died two years later, Fred told his case man-ager that he wanted to go regularly to church again. It was hard for Fred not to have dad and mom around, but the hardest thing was that he was not able to go to church at that first group home. So whenever he is getting ready to go to church now, he tells his friends words that he learned somewhere in the past years, "You know, it's a blessing to go to church." But Fred means it when he says it.

Fred watches the clock in his room on Sunday mornings. He knows that when the little hand on the clock is somewhere by the nine and the big hand is about straight up, it's time to go to the fifteen-passenger van outside his home and start buckling up in the backseat for his ride to church.

This morning at the beginning of their shift the staff decided that Sue Ellen, one of the personal care attendants, will drive today. She has warmed up the vehicle about three or four minutes before Fred works his way to his traditional seat in the back of the van. Dennis will go to the First Baptist Church with Fred, Jeanie, and Salvador and sit with them. Sue Ellen will then drop off two people at Jefferson Avenue Methodist Church where each sits with one of their "circle of friends." She will then take the remaining three with her to St. Joseph's Catholic Church, which is the farthest from the group home. Four other roommates regularly choose not to attend any church, and so Hosea, the third care attendant, will stay home today to care for Sally, Peter, Quintin, and Rosalie.

Fred always gets excited when the van rounds the corner that opens up to a view of the side door of First Baptist Church. Today is no exception. "Oh boy! Oh boy! Go to church! Goody! Go to church!" As the van stops, it is time to make their last check—hair combed, zipper up, buttons buttoned, shoes tied, and a last reminder: "Fred, don't talk in church today."

Fred needs this reminder every Sunday, but each time the words fall on deaf ears. True to form, as Dennis, Salvador, Jeanie, and Fred attempt to sneak in the side door and down the side aisle to the fourth row from the back, Fred spots his cousin Tom "Junior" across the church. Jumping to his feet and waving his hands wildly, Fred shouts across the church sanctuary, "Tom, Tom Junior, it's me Fred! Hi, Tom! Hi, Tom! Over here, Tom! Good to see you, Tom."

Some people in church roll their eyes as Fred shouts his weekly greetings across the sanctuary to his cousin Tom. Many see his waving and talking in church as disturbing to the worship service. Some people would prefer not to have "people like Fred" in church. They especially do not appreciate it when Fred sneaks away from his care attendant and rolls his walker to the front of the church. He somehow ends up next to the pastor as together he and the pastor give the final benediction from the pulpit, with both lifting their hands. Today, at least, Dennis catches and stops Fred before he slips out of the church pew to the front of church.

Lilly Smith is one of a few people who welcomes the regular drama of Fred with his greetings across the sanctuary or his trips up to the pastor. She smiles, knowing how important and significant these routines are to Fred. It is no wonder that Fred searches for her after the service each Sunday morning to give her a hug (or maybe to get a hug from her). He senses that she loves and accepts him just for who he is, and he loves and accepts her in the same way.

A number of years ago Lilly Smith was as frustrated as other church members with Fred's noises, so she decided to talk with him about it. She was concerned that she would not be able to talk with Fred, but it surprised her that Fred was so open and genuine when she asked him why he waved at friends and made so much "noise" at church. Fred told her, "People are important in church and they want to be noticed. I am important too, and I want people to notice me, and I like it when I am in church with God too."

Salvador and Jeanie are not nearly the handful in church as their housemate Fred. People appreciate it that they are not as disruptive as he is, but most keep their distance from all three "people from the home," as they are sometimes referred to. Fred especially is aware that something isn't right when people back away from him and his friends, but he doesn't seem to understand what is happening. Sometimes on the way home from church, he asks Dennis if the people in the church like him or not. "Oh, I know Lilly Smith does," he told Dennis one Sunday morning. "But I don't know if the other church people really like us. They tell us 'hi,' but they look so mean at me, like I did something wrong. I think people need to notice each other and be important to each other. I think that is what God wants, isn't that right, Dennis?" Fred asked.

"That's right, Fred," Dennis responds, but he too is torn between the inappropriateness and appropriateness of Fred's valuable ministry with God's people—if only everyone could see it.

To Think About

1. What are appropriate expressions of God's grace in worship? Who determines what these are? What are the criteria to determine what is appropriate?
2. How willing are we to look at expressions of worship through the eyes and experiences of others who may have much to teach us about the grace of God in worship?
3. What responsibility do people with disabilities have to the rest of the church to behave acceptably in worship? And what responsibility do church members have to love and accept people who may act differently in praising God?
4. What responsibility do you and your church have to include Fred and other people with disabilities into the life of your church?

TWO

"It just ain't right. It ain't fair."

Those parts of the body that seem to be weaker are indispensable, and the parts that we think are less honorable we treat with special honor.

1 Corinthians 12:22–23

Doris is a seventy-three-year-old saint of Jesus Christ. She has been a devoted Christian all her life. When she was very young, she believed that God wanted her to be either a missionary in Africa or a teacher in a Christian school. She studied seriously in elementary and high school and received excellent grades for her efforts. She was even more studious in college, but college was more difficult for her than her earlier schooling. Today she knows the reason she struggled so much in college. Already at the age of eighteen or nineteen she was experiencing the early stages of schizophrenia.

Because of chemistry changes in her brain Doris found it difficult to concentrate on her school work. She began hearing voices—a characteristic of schizophrenia—but she did not dare to tell anyone. She believes that others would have thought her to be demon-possessed and would have rejected her. Doris has lived most of her life in fear of being rejected by others. She even fears, and sometimes even now believes, that God rejects her too. Because of this fear she changed over the next fifty years from a confident, outgoing, enthusiastic person into a shy, retiring woman who has to be drawn into conversations.

Doris did teach a part of one year in a Christian school before it became apparent that she could not continue as a teacher in a classroom. More than fifty years ago she entered a Christian psychiatric hospital, where she was diagnosed as having schizophrenia. She has described her life with schizophrenia in terms of the time "before meds" and the time "after meds." Psychotropic medications have changed her life. Before the introduction of medications, her many hours in counseling convinced her that she had schizophrenia, but did little to make a difference in the quality of her life. At other times in her life shock treatment was the primary approach for schizophrenia. This treatment provided some relief, but it did not significantly make a difference in her life. She was told by well-meaning Christians that she was evil, crazy, or controlled by the devil—none of which is true, but it had a devastating effect on her self-esteem.

Doris has a biochemical disorder that is at the root of her mental illness. All of her adult life she has heard demeaning messages in her head that no one around her is able to hear. But to her they are as clear and real as if a person next to her is speaking. She cannot distinguish between the reality within her and the reality of the world outside of her. Doris also suffers from depression, which complicates her illness of schizophrenia. There have been times in her life when her depression drained her of any motivation to go on living. The biochemical basis for the depression renders any counseling that she has received ineffective. But like medications for schizophrenia, medications for depression have changed her life.

"After meds" has been a miracle for her. She simply feels better about herself, about wanting to enjoy life, and even about those voices she still hears. Doris believes that God really loves her in spite of bouts of moodiness and depression. She knows that she is important to God and she feels that life is a blessing. She likes to write about that. In fact, she writes volumes of material. Every time I come to visit her, she gives me a new envelope with ten to thirty-five pages of her "book."

She writes poetry that expresses the way she sees God caring for her. She writes expository messages about how she understands Scripture and its application to everyday life. She writes about the garden of Eden and the love of Jesus Christ, about the Ten Commandments and the beatitudes. However, what she writes reveals the mental illness she experiences. Her words never make sense. They express random thoughts that hinge together around words that she is thinking about at any given moment. For example, she may start writing her thoughts about the beatitude "Blessed are the poor in spirit." By the time Doris starts writing the word "poor" she is thinking about a "poor little kitten" and "kitten" reminds her of "kitty cat." On paper her sentence reads, "Blessed are the poor little kitten—kitty cat—kitty cats make kitty litter." Nothing Doris writes makes sense to the people who skim through her sheaves of written materials.

The medications have made a tremendous positive impact on her life, but they have not changed the unusual thought patterns of her schizophrenia. Sentences are sometimes arranged in short phrases loosely tied together. Her thoughts appear scattered and unrelated. Even though she often spells words correctly, they do not make sense to an outside reader. But to Doris these "writings" are the masterpiece of her heartfelt relationship to God. She is clearly dedicated to the Lord, but at the same time she is chronically mentally ill and in need of having ongoing care.

Doris loves the time for Bible study. She prepares for her weekly group Bible study, which I have led for persons with mental illness in her home. She makes regular contributions to the discussion of Scripture. Sometimes her insights are profound, and other times they only fit the reality of her inside world. She sings enthusiastically when the old favorites of the church hymnal are sung. In her own way, Doris is a saint who loves her Lord and is greatly loved by her God.

"It just ain't right. It ain't fair," Doris blurted out in a Bible study one Tuesday afternoon. This is so unlike her to be this upset. But because the discussions are lively interchanges in the group, it is easy to move the discussion to whatever it is that is bothering Doris. "What's not fair, Doris?" I asked.

"It's not fair that they won't let me stay in the Sunday morning Bible study at church. Just when I think that people will welcome me in church again, they tell me that I can't come anymore. It just ain't right."

We as a staff have been working hard to normalize the lives of Doris and her roommates. We spent hours with Doris looking for the right church for her. We found one that she decided to join. The pastor and other church leaders were coached so that they could receive Doris as a "regular" member of Christ's body. Doris was looking forward to becoming part of the "community of believers" again. We knew there would be difficulties to overcome.

So it was extremely disheartening to hear Doris's anger and disappointment. At our group home Bible study her words of wisdom are affirmed no matter how off-the-wall her thought patterns might be. But at church people are not so understanding or forgiving of ideas that she expresses—ideas that are sometimes close to the point but at other times don't make sense. We understand that, at home, Doris carries on conversations with the voices in her head. From what she is saying the people at church are petrified that another "Jeffrey Dahmer" might be loose. It becomes apparent that their worst fears are that this "mentally ill" woman who is talking to herself might be a danger to them. It is hard for a church to accept Doris as a "member of Christ's body" when they are afraid. But Doris's lingering behaviors connected to her illness and the church members' old fears result in yet another instance in which God's people miss out on the blessings each can be to the other.

"It ain't fair, Doris," I reflect back to her in that Bible study, thinking that it is not only not fair for Doris but also for the church. Christian mercy and justice don't always get lived out in church, just as they don't always get worked out in society.

I wish I could end this story with a message that the church realizes what is happening and invites Doris back to Sunday school. But this doesn't happen in real life very often. Doris still continues with Bible study, but it is only with her housemates at home. She has stopped going to church worship services altogether now because she believes that church people don't want her. She still writes volumes of spiritual messages and poetry that don't make much sense to the world around her. But I suspect that her writings make perfect sense to God, and he receives all her words of "wisdom" as a sweet, sweet fragrance of praise to him. But it still ain't fair.

To Think About

1. What does it take for the church to bring down its walls for people who don't quite fit in with the rest of God's people?

2. What are you doing personally to make it possible for people like Doris and her friends to be a part of your life so that you and they become real blessings to each other?

3. What might Doris and people like Doris do to be better assimilated into the church?
4. How does the church live out what Paul says in 1 Corinthians 12:22–23: "Those parts of the body that seem to be weaker are indispensable, and the parts that we think are less honorable we treat with special honor"?

Three

"Oh, I could just sing for hours, and I know God would really like it."

I will sing of the LORD's great love forever; with my mouth, I will make your faithfulness known through all generations.

Psalm 89:1

On Tuesdays the hours from 1:00 to 3:00 in the afternoon are the best hours of the week for twenty-eight people with schizophrenia, manic-depressive disorders, panic attacks, and other mental illnesses. These are the hours set aside each week for the people in their foster-care home to sing God's praises together. Some of these people go to church on Sunday, but most do not because they are frightened in crowds and many church people consider them "not with it." But every Tuesday afternoon their hearts ring out in praise to God with as much glee and joy as a church choir experiences on Easter Sunday morning. When David sings, he forgets that he is shy, schizophrenic, and feeling inferior to the rest of the human race.

Wednesday from 10:00 until 11:00 in the morning is the best hour of the week for five elderly, medically fragile and mentally ill people in a home that has been designed for mentally ill persons who have recently been taken out of nursing facilities. "'Tis so sweet to trust in Jesus" is always requested by a woman named June, and she cries as she sings out the words of all three stanzas. She loves it when people come from her church on Sunday to sing. But Wednesday mornings are spent with the chaplain and her housemates. Together they sing the old favorites that have been their spiritual strength throughout the years at mental institutions and nursing homes. Far too often only June and her four friends sing together the spiritual songs that were meant to be shared with all of God's people.

From 7:00 until 8:30 on a Monday, Tuesday, Wednesday, or Thursday evening people with developmental disabilities gather in one or more churches in the community for their best hours of the week. Their Friendship Club is for developmentally disabled persons, and their meetings are filled with singing. Friendship Club pairs a church volunteer with a friend who is developmentally disabled; they meet with other such pairs in groups of ten to thirty people, often in a church basement. This takes place in many areas across the nation. Through these meetings deep and spiritually meaningful relationships are formed. At the meetings the Bible is discussed, a craft project is completed, and the club members pray together; but the heart of Friendship Club is simply Christian friends singing together. And they do it in age-appropriate and developmentally appropriate ways.

On Thursday mornings the public address system announces at the sheltered workshop center that those who wish to come to the Bible story and "sing-along" may come to the cafeteria area from 10:30 until 11:15. People who are profoundly developmentally disabled, those who are physically challenged, and those who experience seizure disorders and/or mental illnesses make their way to the cafeteria for their best hours of the week. Sometimes twenty, thirty, or more people join together to sing praises to God. They know that the time right after morning break will be their time with God for the week.

Kay likes to sing at the program for those with head injuries. Next door at the hospice home for people who are dying of AIDS, cancer, and heart conditions the best hours of the week are when John from a local church comes in and plays the piano. The old favorites of the church bring back memories and focus on the eternal themes of life and death in ways that simple words sometimes fail to do. On Thursday afternoons, Friday mornings, and Sunday afternoons still other groups come together, and again the great hymns of faith or contemporary praise music inspire God's people as they praise him. I am convinced that music is the faith expression of those who are disabled (and maybe of all of God's people). Sometimes when people are unable to utter meaningful sentences or indicate where they stand with the Lord through rational thoughts, they are able to affirm their faith through Christian music. The old favorite hymns of the church, the familiar Sunday school ditties that people have sung to them from birth, the beautiful cantatas, and the majestic Christian classical music are all the means by which they praise God.

"Jesus Loves Me," "Deep and Wide," "I Have a Joy, Joy Down in My Heart," "Amazing Grace," "Blessed Assurance," "Love Lifted Me," "In the Garden," "I Have a Song That Jesus Taught Me," "Great Is Thy Faithfulness," "The Old Rugged Cross," "Do, Lord," "Jesus Keep Me Near the Cross," "Kum Ba Ya," "How Great Thou Art," "Silent Night," "Joy to the World," "Deck the Halls," "Low in the Grave He Lay," "Jesus Christ Is Risen Today," "I Will Sing of the Mercies of the Lord Forever" are only some of the many songs that are sung from memory by people whose meaningful worship of God is in singing.

In my ministry with people with disabilities, I have learned early that providing opportunities for the expression of faith has been most meaningful through music. Whether a chaplain plays a guitar, a keyboard, or an accordion; whether a church youth group conducts a "sing-along" time; whether friends pray, study, do projects together, and sing together in a "friendship club"; whether a Christian volunteer plays a tape recorder or a record player; or whether family members hum and sing "old favorites" in their weekly, monthly, or annual visits, nothing seems to bring God's people closer to their God and tighter in the fellowship of saints than the medium of God-honoring music. Church people need to know what it means for persons with disabilities to join with other Christians in a ministry in which they sing the songs of the redeemed.

This was never so clearly expressed as by David, whom I introduced at the beginning of this chapter. David is mentally ill. He is very shy, but he does talk and express himself when he feels safe with people. When he doesn't feel safe with people, he will blend into the background so that most people think he does not know how to communicate verbally. In fact, some people feel a bit intimidated by him because he goes out of his way to avoid eye contact with others. David happens to wrestle with chronic depression, but he is not much different from June, who is elderly and mentally ill; or Alice, who is blind and developmentally disabled; or Kay, who has had a head injury. They all relate to God through music. David never takes a prominent place in a gathering. He will often wait until everyone else is in the Bible study or "sing-along" and then slip into a back seat where he is sure that no one will notice him, but when he starts to sing, he sings with gusto—from the heart. He sings so intently that he forgets that he is shy, or disabled, or different from other people. All that matters in those moments is that he is praising God.

After a number of years of warming up to David, I had one of those conversations that not many people ever have with him. It came after I had acknowledged how much I appreciated his singing and how much I thought his singing seemed so genuine in its praise to God.

"You know, Reverend Al, I don't know how to do many others things for God. But I can sing. Oh, I could just sing for hours, and I know God would really like it. I think that when we get to heaven, we will be singing all the time too." His words reminded me of the psalmist who wrote and sang: "I will sing of the LORD's great love forever; with my mouth I will make your faithfulness known through all generations" (Ps. 89:1).

To Think About

1. How much of your own expression of faith is expressed through the songs of God's faithfulness and grace?
2. How willing are you to reach out in a music ministry, not just *to* but *with* other people with disabilities in the group home down the street, or the agency across town, or the "Friendship Club" that meets in your church, or maybe even in a church of another denomination?
3. Will you and your church be willing to accept into the church choir people with disabilities who may not always sing exactly on pitch, but who will sing with a zeal that will praise God and bless his people?

Four

"All they see is my wheelchair."

He who began a good work in you will carry it on to completion until the day of Christ Jesus.

Philippians 1:6

Sally is an attractive young woman. Some years ago she was in an automobile accident that left her in a coma for four months and with a brain injury that will continue to give her a lifetime of difficult issues to face. The injury to the front lobes of her brain has caused memory and balance difficulties that she will face for the rest of her life. Most people who first see her never detect that she has had a brain injury. Yet nearly everyone who first notices her sees the wheelchair in which she sits and sometimes reclines between her therapy appointments.

Sally's physical beauty, however, is matched by her inner beauty. Once she had worked through the initial grief of knowing that she would never be able to play sports again and never become the dancer she had hoped to be, Sally developed a perspective toward life that is an inspiration to many around her. Grieving over these losses was painful and difficult for her and, in a real way, it still is. The process of grief continues on for her. But through it she is developing a clear testimony about her relationship with Jesus as her comfort and strength. For a long time Sally has been certain about her relationship to Jesus as her Savior. Her newer insights and realizations have caused her to see Jesus as her loving Lord. With this wisdom Sally's presence exudes life and joy and a sense of adventure.

When Sally first had the accident that smashed her car, the doctor at the rehabilitation center told her family that she would be confined to a wheelchair for the rest of her life. Sally only heard "never walk again" when her parents reported the doctor's prognosis. But from that time on she has been determined that she will walk, and that nothing and no one will stop her from accomplishing this goal.

Sally leaves no stone unturned in her drive to walk and to make the most of her life. No one would dare to suggest anymore that maybe Sally will not accomplish what she sets out to do. We often wonder how much more she will do in her life that she has not already done by this time. She sees a speech therapist, a computer teacher, and a vocational instructor every workday. And she is busy at her church on weekends. Everyone who has met Sally, even once, knows her, and it seems that Sally knows everyone and loves everyone.

The first time I met Sally she was in the hall outside the physical therapy room. It was near the end of a day of intensive therapy sessions for her. She was waiting for her mother to pick her up in the family van, which is specially equipped to carry power wheelchairs. Maybe her guard was down because she was tired, or maybe it was because she had had an unusually bad day, but Sally didn't have her sparkling face on just then.

After the usual chit-chat pleasantries of first introductions, Sally blurted out what was troubling her, and when she had said it, we had to deal with it. Sally had eyed this "hunk of a guy" at church last Sunday, and she was obviously still upset about that experience three days later.

"All he sees when he looks at me is my wheelchair." Her words gushed out about a guy she hoped could be a potential boyfriend. "You know, that's all most people see when they see me," she continued, "they see my wheelchair." Church members were included in her list. Staff members were included, and even I was placed on the list. "I'm just a wheelchair to you" were her parting words.

Certainly Sally was upset, and this was her issue to deal with—not mine. Yet her indictment makes me focus on how I look at not only her but also others with disabilities. Am I talking to Sally the person or Sally the wheelchair? I especially find myself in tension when I see her and others like her as only "the disabled" with whom I work. This rears its ugly head when I make others less than they are and miss the fact that they are fellow image-bearers of God, human beings with feelings and aspirations and abilities. And, as strange as it may seem, I find myself doing the same thing to Sally (and others like her) when I make her *more* than who she is. She is simply another one of God's kids, with aspirations and challenges, with strengths and weaknesses, and with aspects of life that are inspirational alongside aspects that are not put together yet. But Sally is not—she is *not*—a wheelchair. She is not defined by her disability.

I watch so many people in the Christian community who, like me at times, look right past a person like Sally and see only a wheelchair. We may not think we are doing this, but we often focus either on the disability or on making people into someone they are not. For me it sometimes happens when I do not give the person a chance to be real or helpful or meaningful to my life because I have determined that he or she is an object of my service as a "wheelchair-bound" or "sight-limited" or "retarded" or "disabled" person. At other times I have made individuals with disabilities so angelic and wonderful that they are not allowed to live in our world of nosebleeds and scrapes and even crushes on a "real hunk of a guy."

That's what I hear in Sally's words, "You only see my wheelchair. See me. I'm real, and I can do things others can do. There are some things I can't do, but I'm okay. Love me for who I am. Don't confine me to a category, a nonentity."

I also recognize that as penetrating as Sally's words were to me, they said a lot about where she was in her struggles in her personal spiritual journey. Sally herself was wrestling with something very significant when she wondered about what it means for her to be an image-bearer of God. Her self-acceptance and her sense of self-worth are not just someone else's problem, they are also and supremely her problem. Not unlike so many of us who wrestle with self-doubt, Sally was projecting on a boyfriend and on me a battle going on inside her. If I am to see Sally as some*one* and not as some*thing* (a wheelchair), I need to see her pain and struggle and respond to it appropriately.

Soon our conversation focused on issues within her that were driving her. Why was she driving herself so fiercely to walk? Was her outside "wonderfulness" only a façade? Did she see herself as valuable to God? to God's people in the church? or even to herself? The grace of God becomes healing when the painful realities of life are squarely faced and God's forgiveness and love are experienced. What Sally has learned and continues to learn about herself develops her character as a saint in Jesus. There is so much that we have to learn about ourselves, and when we do, God blesses us with new and fresh insights of grace.

Sally is a pretty, fantastic, and insightful young woman. She has a maturity far beyond her nineteen years of life. God is richly blessing her. But she is human. She wrestles deeply with basic life-and-death issues as many of us do. She does not have everything together. She even blows her cool once in a while. But Sally is Sally—an image-bearer of God and one of his kids through Jesus Christ. Sally is not a wheelchair.

To Think About

1. What are the unresolved issues in your life that still need God's healing hand?
2. Do you see individuals with disabilities as people first of all?
3. How can you enter into the pain of another person's life and see him or her as real?
4. How willing are you to be vulnerable with others so that God can touch you and them with his grace?

Five

"Go to work now."

Cast all your anxiety on him because he cares for you.

1 Peter 5:7

John was beside himself. The work coach at a Hope Network sheltered workshop was as frustrated as John in their inability to communicate with each other. The more upset John became, the more his volume intensified and the more the speed of his conversation increased and the more difficult it was to understand him. It is always difficult to understand John, but the difficulty is increased whenever he becomes agitated and talks more rapidly. The seven other people with developmental disabilities in his group were assembling cardboard boxes for a local container manufacturer. It was a "rush job," and the job coach was noticing that John's problem was influencing his workmates.

"Chaplain, can you come right over to our group?" John's coach sounded desperate on the telephone. I don't get many calls like that as a chaplain, so I knew that something must be quite wrong for the job coach to call. "John's out of control, and I need to get the other guys to settle down. We have a hot job that has to get out, but with John being as upset as he is we can't get the work out. Please come as soon as you can and try to find out what's wrong."

I couldn't believe that it was John who was so upset. Peter maybe; Sally sometimes. But not John. John has Down's syndrome. He is always the first one to greet me when I come to his place of employment. He always gets to work on time in the morning; he's the last to leave at the end of the day and the one who has to be dragged away from his job at break time. John is not a troublemaker, and rarely is he upset about anything. His problem (identified on the plan of correction set up for him), if it can even be called a problem, is that he believes he has to shake the hand of everyone who comes within sight. Even at his church he is the self-appointed greeter of new people who come to worship.

His plan of correction was set up to help him understand when it is appropriate to greet people and when it is repetitious or unnecessary to shake the hands of others.

"..ello, I ain't fine. ..ow ..r ..oou? (Hello, I ain't fine. How are you?)" John greeted me when I came to his workplace. It was a bit different from his standard greeting to everyone that frequently beams from his lips and face. "..ello, I'm fine. ..ow ..r ..oou?"

So I understood right away that even from John's perspective something big was bothering him. But then John was making more sounds I didn't recognize. He was trying to tell me something. As much as I wanted to, I just could not understand him. It frustrated me to see John getting so upset with me because I didn't understand what he was saying. For a few minutes the job coach sat with us too as we tried to decipher his words, but the job coach soon had to excuse himself to be with the others at their rush job.

John was determined to make clear to me what he wanted me to know. *I need to hang in there with him,* I kept thinking to myself. *Besides, isn't this what Jesus would want me to do?* But I was not able to get what he was saying. How could I help him to get through to me?

"Slow down, John. I'm going to listen real closely. But you have to talk slowly, really slowly. Say your words one at a time." I spoke as slowly and deliberately as I was requesting him to do.

So John started over again. And again, and again. Somewhere in that early conversation I heard the word "hospital." Later, I was not sure but another word that sounded like "brother" came out. "Did you say, 'hospital . . . brother'?" I asked him.

"Ya, Ya," was his clear message, but then more sounds came and eventually " . . . brother . . . hospital . . . knee . . . op'ration. . . ." Slowly, ever so slowly the words came together. It took an hour before I heard the words, "Brother, hospital, knee operation, St. Mary's. *Pray!*"

At last I put it together. "You want me to pray for your brother who is having a knee operation at St. Mary's Hospital?"

"Ya! Ya!" his mouth uttered and his head nodded.

John and I prayed together for his brother, for the doctors and nurses who would be God's servants to be used in the healing of his brother's knee. It didn't make any difference to John that all his friends saw us pray in the middle of the work floor. He was doing what he knew he had to do before he could get into his work. "Pray for my brother. Put him in God's hands. Ask God to bless the doctors. They can only do their work with God's help" seemed to be what John was telling me with the few words I heard.

John assumed a posture for prayer that he learned at home or maybe at his church. Eyes closed, hands folded together and pointed to heaven. He made noises that sounded like "Amen" after the petitions I offered to God. I thought to myself that God was listening closely to two of his people praying together.

But John startled me with his words after our prayer. They were words that I have reflected on for a long time since that day we were praying in the middle of the sheltered workshop. John opened his eyes, unclasped his hands, and began wiping his hands together. His frustration was gone. The same old smiling face was back. His words were filled with faith and confidence. I'm sure I heard him say, "Go to work now."

Would that I felt that strongly about the need to pray for my brother as he faces an operation! Would that I would be so bold about getting someone to pray for him! Would that I could be so unashamed about praying so publicly! Would that I could turn my worries over to the Lord and let them go as confidently as John did.

John still greets me whenever I come to his work area. When I last asked him about his brother, I heard, "..e's fine. ..ow ..r ..oou? ..e's fine." And I know that if John knew that I were to go into the hospital, he'd probably be upset again until he could find someone who would listen.

"Chap'in Al, hospital . . . operation . . . *pray!*"

To Think About

1. How important is it for you to pray for people who have a special need?
2. Are you confident enough to pray unashamedly before others?
3. Can you so turn your worries to the Lord that they no longer bother you?
4. How much are you aware that your disabled brothers and sisters in the faith are praying for you?

Six

"I thank God for you."

I thank my God every time I remember you.

Philippians 1:3

Jane's memorial service was one of the first funerals I conducted as a chaplain to disabled people. I had known Jane as one of many individuals in the behavioral treatment center, which provides day treatment for persons whose disabling conditions include severe behavioral problems. Jane would often pick at her face and obsessively open up wounds on both her face and arms. At the day treatment program she would sometimes scream from nine in the morning till she left at three in the afternoon. We might learn that the entire previous night she had been screaming at her group home as well, exhausting the staff working with her on two shifts. At other times she would sit quietly in the background developing her hand-eye coordination by placing pegs in appropriate openings. Because she could not tell us what was wrong, we could only guess what was really going on inside her.

Jane was not an easy person to try to help. Anything could set her off into one of her many temper tantrums. If one of the other people at either her group home or the day-care center became agitated, Jane would have another one of her bad days. If the ride in the van between her group home and the center was in any way different from the routine, she was set off, and those who worked with her knew that they would have another very tiring day.

Even so, Jane was very much loved by everyone. As difficult as she was to work with sometimes, everyone who worked with her loved her deeply because she had endearing qualities that drew out the best in case managers, residential aides, activity instructors, and even a chaplain like me. She knew a lot of songs, but one that we would sing together even in the midst of one of her temper tantrums was "Jesus loves me, this I know. For the Bible tells me so."

Then Jane died. She died suddenly and quite unexpectedly. In the middle of the night after several days of having major temper tantrums, she just stopped breathing! She was gone! We think now that she was hurting very badly during those days but did not have any way to let us know what was wrong. Immediately we began making phone calls to literally dozens of people—both her paid caregivers and her friends.

Jane's sudden death was a shock to us, but as we who knew her best began to reflect more on her going, we came to realize that it was her unusual life that made the greatest impact on us. She demanded much from us, and her death was a powerful reminder of how much she meant to us. Our tears flowed, not because we were relieved to see her gone, but because we loved her and she had meant so much to us.

One of our staff members suggested that a memorial service for Jane would be a way to share our grief and seek God's comfort in our loss. I am very thankful to the person who made this suggestion because it was the first in an ongoing

number of memorial and funeral services I have been conduct-
ing for people with disabilities on a regular basis. At first we
decided to invite only those people who had provided care for
Jane and maybe a few people with disabilities who would
understand what was happening. Then the list grew to an ever-
wider number of people who loved Jane and had worked with
her in the state hospital where she had been for seventeen years
before any of us knew her. I have come to realize that unless we
use appropriate ways to express grief, all of us, and especially
those of us with disabilities, miss out on receiving God's healing grace in the painful realities of death.

Finally, in our process of trying to remember all those who
knew Jane, one staff person remembered that on some obscure
chart were the names of her parents. We discovered that they
still lived here in town. Certainly we needed to invite them too.

We learned that her parents had come only once to the
group home while she lived there, and that was four years earlier when she had first come from the state hospital. They had
never been to the day-care program. But not much more was
known about them. When we finally found the right telephone
number, we informed them about their daughter's death and
invited them to the memorial service. They said they very
much wanted to come. And it was at that service that a powerful story of God's grace unfolded.

The memorial service was held at 3:30 in the afternoon at
the behavioral day center because it was the only place large
enough to hold everyone who indicated they wanted to be
there. We chose the time of 3:30 as this would allow the night
staff at the group home to have had a night's sleep, the day center staff could have all their people with disabilities shuttled off
to their homes, case managers from other agencies could have

finished their daily tasks, and, perhaps most important, Jane's parents could be there as well.

I counted them. There were sixty people present at the memorial service. Eight were people with disabilities. Two were Jane's mother and father. And fifty were Jane's closest friends—*all* of whom were paid professionals who had grown to love her and now missed her dearly. Even administrators from three different agencies were present, because they, like the others, had in one way or another been affected by Jane's life and ministry to them.

I selected Philippians 1:3–5 for the words from Scripture to reflect on in that memorial service. "I thank my God every time I remember you. In all my prayers for all of you, I always pray with joy because of your partnership in the gospel."

I can't tell you why, but I firmly believed then as I firmly believe now that Jane shared a partnership in the gospel with me. She had a ministry. And I thank God every time I remember her.

And apparently at that memorial service, many other people also thanked God for her. Story after story of Jane's little touches of grace came out. The big hug from Jane to the night aide who was so frustrated with her during a series of screaming spells, the hardly noticeable appreciation Jane gave her van driver when the driver helped her off the van and into the center, the "Jesus loves me" song that was mouthed to me in my ministry with her, Jane's enticing nonverbal challenge to herself to do more and better things than a support staff believed she was capable of doing. . . . So much appreciation for Jane and for how God used her to minister to us.

At the service and in the front row of the room were Jane's dad and mom taking in these words of appreciation for their daughter. Tears were soon streaming from their eyes. When others stopped talking, Jane's father stood up. It was hard for him to speak between his tears of joy and tears of sadness mixed in that bittersweet moment.

Dad talked of a day when this beautiful little baby girl was born. She was the joy of their lives. But they learned even before she was taken out of the hospital that their daughter had major problems because of the birthing process and would never be normal. But they loved Jane. Because their faith in Jesus also included realizing that God's promises of salvation were also for their daughter, they made promises to God to do their best in bringing her up in the Lord as they brought her to be baptized.

For several years they kept Jane at home and cared for her. Some time before she was four and at a time when the responsibility to care for her was most intense, their doctor suggested that it would be best for Jane and for them to send her to the Children's Retreat at Pine Rest Christian Hospital. Many, many other very young children would also be at the center. They decided to follow the doctor's advice and take her there. At first they visited her daily, then weekly, and eventually monthly. They were happy that the Christian staff sang songs like "Jesus loves me," "This little light of mine," and "He's got the tiny little baby in His hand" to their daughter.

Eventually Jane's behavioral needs and her very costly care became reasons why they had to make the painful decision to transfer her to a state institution for "people like her." First she was sent to a state hospital a great distance from home. Later she was transferred to a regional center closer to home. Her parents visited her more frequently at first, but as they became older, it was harder for them to do so. One of their consolations was that Jane always seemed to become endeared to many people and she always seemed to bring out the very best character of her caregivers. As her dad related his story, he told of hearing that she had come out of the regional center, had come back to their hometown, and was living in the group home. They were old now, but they did see their daughter once. They saw that she was well cared for. They had told themselves when they made the visit that, as they had been told many years before, it was probably best that they not visit their daughter again.

As Jane's father told his story, tears were streaming down his face. "I'm not so sure that it was best for Jane," he added, "and I'm not so sure that it was best for us that we haven't had more to do with her. We made this decision because we at one time thought that this is what God wanted for our daughter. But now when I sit here at this memorial service and hear how many fond memories all of you have of our daughter, and when I think of the many ways she ministered to you, I think we missed out on a whole lot."

Jane is remembered by many of us as a gift God gave us, a gift who in her needy person and her strangely alluring personality was used by God to develop our lives and ministries. Even though the memorial service was a time in which God was praised and Jane's life was remembered, her father's parting words to the fifty-eight of the rest of us at the service were extremely powerful.

"And I thank God for all of you too."

To Think About

1. Who are the most challenging people in your life and how has God used them to mold you to be the kind of person you are?

2. How have some of the most trying times in decision making driven you closer to the Lord and made you more reliant on him?

3. In what ways can gratitude to the Lord be expressed in your most perplexing circumstances?
4. For whom are you grateful to God?
5. To what extent are you willing to be vulnerable to the challenges of persons like Jane and to allow them to minister to you?

Seven

"That would give us a great time in the Word."

For the word of God is living and active. Sharper than any double-edged sword, it penetrates even to dividing soul and spirit, joints and marrow; it judges the thoughts and attitudes of the heart.

Hebrews 4:12

When Bob finishes his job at the grocery store at 3:00 in the afternoon, he sometimes runs the three miles from work to his home. Some days he is running because he is on the verge of a panic attack. On other days, in his schizophrenia he hears voices that are making unusual demands of him. On these days Bob wants to avoid meeting anyone. But on Tuesday afternoons he runs home for another reason. On Tuesdays he wants to be back in time for his Bible study at 4:30. He often worries that he is demon-possessed, especially when he is petrified with a panic attack or feels out of control with the voices, but, no matter what, he does not want to miss important time in the Word of God, when he and his four or more friends faithfully attend a Bible study.

Bob is a student of the Scripture. He spends hours studying the Word as part of his commitment of faith in Jesus Christ—a commitment he made early in his life. He also seeks answers and comfort from Scripture as he faces the panic attacks, which he calls the "scare attacks," and the voices that professionals have identified as the result of schizophrenia. Bob has difficulty with these diagnoses; he is certain that the devil is taunting him. He has come to realize that he is better when he takes the medications the doctor prescribes for him to deal with these situations. He longs for the time when he will not have to take the medications, even though he must take them for the rest of his life.

Every afternoon Joseph comes to the same home after work, but he arrives an hour earlier than Bob. He arrives home by 2:30 in the afternoon because he works across the street from their home for people with mental illnesses. Joseph too has schizophrenia. He needs the more structured work environment of a sheltered workshop because he experiences more difficulty with the outside world than his friend Bob does. But when he arrives home on Tuesday afternoons, he compulsively engages in a set of chores that he believes are necessary before he can attend the 4:30 Bible study.

Joseph frequently seeks God's will by randomly reading a text that pops out to him as he simply opens the Bible and reads what is before him. The Bible study hour on Tuesday afternoon is one event to which he looks forward every week. He believes that it helps him stay focused on God and how God wants him to live.

Tom also finds it hard to wait until Tuesday afternoon. He takes the bus from across town where he washes dishes at a restaurant. He often has to hustle to get home on time to make the Bible study. Tom was not raised with the Bible, but many years ago he started reading and studying the Bible in a state institution for the mentally ill when a chaplain first introduced him to the Bible. Tom has a photographic memory and over the years has become an encyclopedia of Bible knowledge. He has become our "walking concordance" in the Bible study group.

Tom has difficulty with what appears to be contradictions in Scripture. He will often bring them up when we are in our Bible study together. Because he experiences paranoia connected to his mental illness he sometimes has outbursts of anger at others and at God during our studies. But after a flare-up he feels guilty and worries about his salvation. Over and over again he is looking for the assurance of his salvation while struggling with passages of Scripture that seem to give different and contradictory messages. So Bible study is vital for his daily life but in a quite different way from that of the other members of the group. He spends much time before a Bible study familiarizing himself with other Scripture texts that complement the passage we will be studying together.

Kevin does not work at all. He is in the day program of the group home in which he and his other friends reside. His mental illness and speech impairments make it very difficult for others to understand what he is thinking. Kevin has definite opinions about the Bible passages we study, but he often becomes frustrated when we do not grasp what he is saying. He often comes to the Bible study for a while, and then when he has tried to talk without success, he will leave, only to return for short periods of time to check on the progress and content of the study. What is amazing about Kevin's contribution to the Bible study is his ability to read the Scripture aloud prior to the study of the passage. When he reads Scripture, he shows absolutely nothing of the speech impediment of his regular conversation. So he takes great delight in reading the Bible passage as we start our studies.

George also makes sure he catches the early bus to get home from his day job on Tuesday afternoons to make it to

Bible study on time. He has generally worked seven hours on an assembly line before arriving home. He was raised as a Roman Catholic, and as a child he did not read or study the Bible. But today the Scripture is his spiritual lifeblood. The decisions of Vatican II in the 1960s have made a big difference in his personal relationship with the Lord, especially as God's Word was made available to him by his church. He is proud of his New Jerusalem Bible, which he purchased from his church bookstore. His priest comes to visit George every month for communion. He has encouraged him to continue with the Bible study because he sees how much George has grown with his study of the Word. I believe that George would be at the Bible study even if the priest did not encourage him to do so because it has become so important to him.

George too is being treated for schizophrenia, and he is aware of how successful his treatment is with the newer medications he is taking. Occasionally the medications don't work in quite the same way for him. Then for a period of time he is very unsure of himself—until his psychiatrist adjusts his medications. He acknowledges often in the study of God's Word that his Healer is really God, who uses the medications to accomplish healing. George is utterly serious about wanting to learn as much as he can from the Bible about his Jesus.

Roger is the most recent newcomer to Bible study. He has been attending these meetings for only nine months or so. Most of the others have been in the Bible study for six or seven years. It is obvious from his familiarity with the Scripture that Roger has spent much time in the Bible before coming to the group home. Roger has a long history of having seizures more than once a day. This is why he was sent to the same group home as the others. Like George and the others, he is taking the newer medications that help him live a reasonably normal life. He hasn't had a seizure in months. He attributes his lack of having seizures to God's answering his prayers and God's blessing of making available newer and more effective medication. Roger also spends time before the Bible lesson studying the Bible verses for that day.

We are studying the book of Hebrews. I don't remember who suggested some months ago that this be the next book of the Bible for us to study, but immediately others chimed in: "Hebrews has so much to offer us about our faith." "That book is really challenging." "I haven't studied Hebrews before but it should give us a great time in the Word." What I remembered about Hebrews is that it is a difficult book for most Christians to understand. We had already studied Philippians, Galatians, Ephesians, James, 1 and 2 Peter, and the book of Acts. I really wondered if these men had any idea what kind of Bible study they were getting themselves into.

But they do have an idea of what they are studying. They are willing to dig deeper into what the Bible says, what it means, and how to apply it to their lives than I have found many people in church groups willing to do. I suspect it would surprise many people outside this circle of people with mental illnesses that five or six persons with schizophrenia can have an in-depth study of the Bible. Yet I know that these men would not miss their Tuesday afternoons studying Hebrews for anything.

The study of Hebrews 4 on one Tuesday afternoon was especially powerful because each person had something to say about the passage that reflected his or her own life experiences. "For the word of God is living and active. Sharper than any double-edged sword, it penetrates even to dividing soul and spirit, joints and marrow; it judges the thoughts and attitudes of the heart" from Hebrews 4:12 were the words before us.

Kevin read the passage clearly and distinctly, but when he tried to tell us what he thought the Bible was saying, he spoke with such difficulty that none of us could really understand what he was saying. Tom, the walking concordance of the Old and New Testament, reminded us that according to Psalm 119:11 the Word of God is hidden in our hearts that we might not sin against him. He asked, "Could it be that God is preventing me from doing wrong when I read the Bible and am not able to forget what I read?" Bob told us about how "double-edged" the Bible has been for him—sometimes making him feel so guilty for the times he has been sinfully wrong and other times making him feel so affirmed and good because he is saved. Roger, on the other hand, wondered if his study of the Bible penetrated into his joints and bones and was the reason he no longer experiences seizures. George again remarked about how good he feels when he studies the Bible because when God is doing this penetrating and judging stuff, he is making him better. Sometime during the discussion Joseph opened his Bible to John 1 and began reading, "In the beginning was the Word, and the Word was with God, and the Word was God. He was with God in the beginning." And with the rhetoric of a high church mass he ended by saying, "This is the word of the Lord. In the name of the Father, Son, and Holy Spirit."

In this group home God's people come to be students of the Word on Tuesday afternoons. Sometimes the wisdom spoken is brilliant; at other times it is not wisdom at all. But the time in the Word is time when God's grace abounds. As important as the Scripture and the insights that each person contributes to the study are, it is what God is doing to and with the character of each one that becomes another lesson in grace in the Tuesday afternoon Bible class.

To Think About

1. What blessings have you received from Christians who have quite different backgrounds, denominations, perspectives, even different mental illnesses? How do you think this diversity can make the study of Scripture so rich?

2. Are you willing to step out of your comfort zone to experience the joy of studying Scripture with persons with disabilities in a home near yours?

3. How can you encourage groups of people at work or at church to be students of the Word of God?

4. What evidences of Christian character building do you get out of being with other Christians in Bible study?

Eight

"Today's my birthday."

If one part [of the body of Christ] is honored, every part rejoices with it.

1 Corinthians 12:26

Today's my birthday," Colleen announced as I arrived at the sheltered workshop where she was working. Three weeks ago when I went to her group home to visit, I heard her tell me the same thing. And when I happened to see her at her church several months ago, I overheard her tell someone else the same thing. Certainly she did not have three birthdays in the past six months.

Colleen is only one of many people with whom I have a specialized ministry who regularly, if not daily, call attention to their "birthdays." Many times when Colleen and others alert us to their birthdays, they are simply engaging in attention-seeking behavior. When I respond to this behavior by conversing on the birthday theme, I only reinforce this method of getting attention. There are many of these attention-seeking behaviors that Colleen and her friends use that I have learned not to reinforce lest I help them fall into a self-defeating interchange with people.

For instance, John, one of Colleen's friends, told me once that he was going to the hospital the next day. I believed him and asked him why was he going to the hospital. "Surgery," he replied. "I'm going to have surgery." In the conversation that followed I learned what kind of surgery he was going to have and when it was going to be. I asked, among other things, if he wanted me to pray for him and visit him in the hospital. All this sounds innocent enough, but John was not scheduled for surgery at all. As I found out later, what started out as a way to get my attention and keep him from doing his job turned into a whole series of lies that he had to manufacture—all because I didn't catch on to what he was trying to do. His pretense accomplished the end of getting my attention and providing him an excuse for not doing a job that he was assigned to do. But it also left him with the guilt of telling me a whole set of untruths. These lies had to be covered with other lies after I showed up at the hospital the next day and discovered his ruse. Needless to say, when I checked back with him, I was not quite as ready to believe him when he told me that a policeman took him to jail so that he couldn't go to the hospital. So his attention-seeking behavior left me feeling irked with him and wanting to discount whatever he would tell me in the future.

When Colleen says, "Today's my birthday" and does so repeatedly, I see it for the most part as attention-seeking behavior and do not respond to her for some of the same reasons I don't quickly respond to John. But I received a new insight one day when Colleen told me for the hundredth time, "Today's my birthday." In an attempt to redirect her attention from what I believed to be "attention-seeking" behavior, I responded to Colleen, "That's nice. What's that you're doing today?"

"No, today is my birthday. It really is." "Yea, sure it is. Isn't that a new blouse you are wearing?" I stumblingly ask so as to not reward this obvious attention-seeking behavior. "Sure is. I got this pretty blouse for my birthday." As if I am really dense and don't have a sensitive bone in my body, Colleen puts it to me once again. "You don't believe me, do you? I have a birthday today, and my parents gave me this blouse as my birthday gift."

"Da! It *is* your birthday, isn't it?" I responded. "Sorry. You've told me that so many times that I didn't believe you anymore. Happy birthday, Colleen." But I thought to myself, *That's the problem with this attention-seeking behavior. A person cries wolf so many times that when the wolf is really there, no one takes the person seriously. That is certainly Colleen's problem, but maybe I need to take some ownership in the problem too.*

"Colleen, I really want to celebrate the fact that it is your birthday today. But I am having a hard time doing so because you told me so many times that it's your birthday that I don't believe you anymore. Have you ever noticed that other people don't pay any attention anymore when you tell them it's your birthday?" She nods. Then I asked her, "Why do you think you do it all the time?"

Colleen didn't reply right away, but then she said, "I like it when people come to my birthday. I like it when I get presents. I like it when people think I'm important. I like it when I feel like I belong. I guess I want to feel that way all the time. So maybe that's why I want my birthday all the time."

What Colleen really craves deep within her is to be included in what we Christians call the "community of believers." "If one part suffers, every part suffers with it; if one part is honored, every part rejoices with it" (1 Cor. 12:26). But her attention-seeking behaviors make it impossible for her to achieve the thing she wants most. I suspect that she is not able to realize that her deep desire to belong can be fulfilled in Christ's bringing his people together as a body. I wonder how many other Christians are able to make the connection of this inner yearning to feel important and included and honored to Jesus' calling us together to be his bride. And I also wonder what self-defeating, attention-seeking behaviors we may have that interfere with our life as a "community of Christians."

"Colleen, I believe what you say is really important," I told her. "I want other people to think that I am important too. I like it too when other people like me and like to do things with me, and I like it when I feel that I belong and am needed. So what you want when you tell me it's your birthday is right on. I think it's what Jesus wants us to have too. That's why he gives us people to love us, people who are also Christians. And that's why he gives us the church. But you know, Colleen. I don't think telling everyone that it's our birthday all the time gets us what we want so badly. We'll have to come up with a better way to let each other know that God loves us and we are important to him and to each other."

I think that is what I said to Colleen that day. Certainly that is what I wanted to say. But I am not sure what she heard or really understood, because the next time I saw her, she told me, "Today's my birthday."

"Colleen, God loves you. I love you. You are really important. You belong to God."

"But today really is my birthday." Self-defeating behaviors die hard. Or, is it really her birthday this time?

To Think About

1. Do you see self-defeating, attention-seeking behaviors in yourself that compare to those of Colleen?
2. What insights do Colleen's words give you about the nature and purpose of the church of Christ?

3. How do these self-defeating aspects of our lives really get changed? I suspect that most of us have as much difficulty changing as Colleen apparently did. What responsibility do we have to speak with each other about these behaviors we observe in each other?

Nine

"God teaches me patience."

Be joyful in hope, patient in affliction, faithful in prayer.

Romans 12:12

I introduced myself to the religion editor from the newspaper. We met in front of Eric's apartment building at one o'clock in the afternoon as we had arranged. It was nearing Easter, and the editor wanted to have a dynamic human-interest story as his Easter lead story. Eric was waiting for us in his two-bedroom apartment, which is especially designed to meet the needs of a person who has mobility impairments and lives independently with occasional help from personal-care attendants. One of his attendants had been with him for four hours prior to our arrival just to get him ready for this important afternoon.

Eric's good friend, Neil, had contacted the editor several weeks before and suggested that Eric's story would make a great human interest story for the religion section of our local newspaper. The editor had then contacted me when he heard I had been making pastoral calls on Eric for several years. He asked if I would help him communicate with Eric for a feature article in the newspaper.

Eric is mostly paralyzed from his neck down because of a vicious attack on his life some years before. He can't speak through his larynx because his vocal cords had been destroyed in that attack. Now he spends most of his life in his small apartment. To get the interview for the feature story, the editor had to come to Eric's apartment and work through another person to communicate with him by means of a unique letter-board arrangement.

As we arrived at Room 109, I knocked at Eric's door with my usual but unique rap signifying to my friend that I am the guest at his door. His door opened as if by magic. But it was not magic; Eric had triggered the mechanism that opened the door by bumping a switch pad on his powered wheelchair with his head. When he is not in his chair, this triggering pad is placed on his bed near his left ear.

Eric's head movement against the pad is part of the adaptive equipment that makes it possible for him to live relatively independently. To open the door for us he triggered the pad past the first stage of a mechanism that turns on his radio; past the second stage, which engages his telephone answering system; past the third stage, which lights up his computer system; and even beyond a fourth stage, which controls his television. It was with the fifth movement against the switch pad that Eric engaged the motor that opened the hallway door to his apartment and invited us in.

Eric shared his life story with the reporter that afternoon. He used a letter board that he had devised first with the help of nurses at the nursing home and later revised with a speech therapist. The letter board contains letters of the alphabet and single-digit numbers arranged in six lines. His computer, which is often broken, is another means of communication he sometimes uses to "speak" with people, but it too works in much the same way as his letter board. Every thought, every word is slowly and carefully spelled out, letter by letter.

At the interview I became the mediator through whom Eric communicated with the reporter. Eventually, even the reporter learned to use the letter board to communicate directly with Eric. "Row one," I announced, and Eric's eyes rolled upward. "E-A-R-D," I continued, and again his eyes lifted. "Eric, your first letter is D. Row one, row two." Eric signaled again. "Row two: T-O," and again he let me know the next letter was "O, that is DO." If I had continued with the letters, row two letters on the letter board would have included "T-O-I-L-G-K." Row three contain the letters N-S-F-Y-X, row four H-C-P-J, row five M-W-Q, and row six B-Z-0-1-2-3-4-5-6.

"Row one, row two." Eric's eyes rolled upward again and eventually he signaled a "U" for "you." "Do you?" I reminded myself. "Row one, row two, row three, row four, row five," and again Eric's eyes lifted. "M-W." Eric acknowledged that the next letter was "W." Each letter was painstakingly spelled out by Eric. "DO YOU WANT COFFEE?" he eventually asked. When we agreed, his eyes again sent a message to his personal-care attendant who is even more adept than we at reading him and his gestures. His message was clear, "Please serve my guests coffee."

As we drank our coffee, the painstakingly slow but clear story of Eric's life unfolded. Eric told us, "YOU JUST WON'T BELIEVE HOW GOOD GOD IS." The message was written in shorthand by the editor and eventually put into print for the Western Michigan readers to read: "GOD BROUGHT ME OUT OF DEATH. GOD IS USING MY DISABILITY SO THAT OTHER PEOPLE WILL LISTEN IN A WAY THEY WOULD NOT IF I WERE ABLE BOD-IED. GOD IS REALLY GOOD."

Ten years before our visit, Eric had been a thirty-five-year-old enterprising owner of a construction company. He had a bright future as a successful, black businessman in Detroit, Michigan. But one evening an employee high on cocaine came to Eric after work with every intention of stealing money from him. In the craze of the moment, the man took a screwdriver and stabbed Eric behind his right ear and in the throat. In twisting motions the attacker injured Eric's larynx, his spinal cord, and parts of his brain that affect his ability to use his legs and arms. He then stole Eric's money and left him for dead. Eric tells us how he remembers blacking out and believing that he would die.

Eric woke up from his coma three months later. He was lying in a bed in a nursing home, paralyzed from the neck down and totally unable to speak. The nursing staff thought he was a living vegetable without the ability to think, communicate, or function for himself. But Eric's eye and head movements revealed something different. He was able to roll his eyes upward and nod his head slightly, especially if he did not like his food or if he disagreed with a passerby's opinion. There was obviously much more going on inside this person whose body could not move and whose eye and head movements were ever so slight. One nurse caught on to these movements and experimented with him.

"One blink of the eyes means 'yes' and two blinks is a 'no,'" she suggested. Much to most people's amazement Eric would affirm his nurse's requests and intentions with a single blink of the eyes and show his disapproval or disagreement with two blinks. Even the slight nods of agreement and sideways motions of disagreement became the early means of communication between Eric and the outside world. This was the beginning of what is now a lifetime of recovering and adapting to new challenges for him.

Eric knew the Lord before he was attacked, but the reality of God's grace became real from the very moment he came out of the coma. He told the reporter that even when no one thought he could think or communicate, he leaned on the Lord. At first he was horrified to think that he would be totally isolated from other people inside the walls of his body, and yet God by his grace was there for him. When Eric first learned to communicate by blinking his eyes, he felt tremendous gratitude to his Savior and Lord, even while struggling to make others understand him. When he was first placed in a wheelchair and could look around at others, when he devised a communication system with a speech therapist, and while he persevered through hours and weeks and months and even years of never-ending rehabilitation training, his eyes reflected the gratitude of a man overflowing with God's grace.

Eric let the reporter and me know that because of his disability he found himself depending entirely on the grace of God. The words in the newspaper reflected Eric's conversation, spelled out letter by letter from the letter board: "WITH MY DISABILITY I HAVE COME TO LEARN TO DEPEND ON THE LORD AND ON OTHER PEOPLE. I THINK THIS INTERDEPENDENCE ... IS A PART OF THE GOSPEL MESSAGE."

This is not to say that Eric is not lonely. He is often lonely, and he is the first to let others know that life has many bleak moments for him. He often describes his life as being "in the prison house of [his] body." He frequently becomes depressed, especially when for weeks he has no visitors other than the personal-care attendants who come for short periods of time in the morning, at lunch time, and in the evening to provide for his basic bodily care. He misses his family who live three hours away in Detroit. He easily gets irritated with people when they don't live up to his expectations.

Eric jumps at the opportunity to talk via his letter board or with his computer to church groups, seminary students, and anyone who will listen to him. His computer has a voice synthesizer that speaks for him to groups of people, but more often than not the computer doesn't operate as it should. Eric has also taken the opportunity to "march" his wheelchair before government officials to plead the cause of individuals who are disabled. He has a keen sense of justice and often stands out for decency and fairness in behalf of persons who have been given a raw deal.

The reporter from the newspaper asked Eric in the interview, "What has been one of the greatest things you have learned from all your experiences?" Eric thought of the many, many things that have been important to him. At other times he might have given answers in terms of the grace of God or God's power made perfect in his weakness. But his answer this time was simple and very powerful. It became the theme of the reporter's Easter human-interest story: "PATIENCE! GOD IS TEACHING ME PATIENCE."

I thought of my own times with Eric and the things I have learned about God's grace from him. Certainly, the fruit of the Holy Spirit called patience is a fruit I too learned from God through the ministry of my friend Eric. The root word for "patience" in the Greek New Testament is "endurance." Certainly Eric has endured and persevered, and in that sense he has learned from the Holy Spirit that marvelous fruit called patience. And it is God's gift of patience that allows him to live by the grace of Jesus Christ.

To Think About

1. How have you experienced God's power made perfect in your weakness?

2. In what ways are you willing to open yourself up to a ministry by a person like Eric, who has much to teach you simply because of his total dependence on God and other people?
3. How have you experienced the fruit of the Holy Spirit called *patience* as it is taught by the experience of *endurance*?
4. How have you experienced God's grace in your personal weaknesses and challenges?

Ten

"Hey, everybody! I am crying too. My mom died!"

Why are you downcast, O my soul? Why so disturbed within me? Put your hope in God, for I will yet praise him, my Savior and my God.

Psalm 42:11

Catherine, now sixty years old, has lived a lifetime of secrets. Most people she knows today do not have any idea of what her life has been like. Maybe her lead residential aide, who studied her case record more closely than most other people, has some knowledge of her life before she came to this home for people who experience profound developmental disabilities. Certainly her eighty-five-year-old mother, who comes to see her at the group home every few months, knows her former experiences the best. But most other people have neither the interest nor the time to learn about them.

Catherine cannot tell others what her life has been like. She now lives in a type A group home for developmentally disabled people with five other men and women who, like her, are profoundly retarded. She cannot talk; she cannot walk; and she cannot feed herself. But sixteen full- and part-time people work with her for three shifts a day, twenty-one shifts a week. They have learned to read her nonverbal language and are able to interpret her wants and wishes through her smiles, crying sounds, temper tantrums, and the other behavioral indicators. But even they do not know the many secrets of what it was like for her to live in the mental-health system for nearly fifty-five years.

If she could talk, what stories would Catherine tell? Would they be stories of mother and dad in the great depression of the 1930s as they went through the agony of giving their baby up to "the system" before she even knew what was happening to her? Would they be stories about living in large dormitories of state regional centers where there were only a few attendants to spread their love thinly to a roomful of people? Or would they be stories of attendants who would take their frustrations out on people like Catherine with verbal, physical, and even sometimes sexual abuse? Would she tell stories of long periods of loneliness and meaninglessness? What stories would she tell of pleasure, quality love, and meaningful relationships in her sixty years? If only she could talk!

Those who know how to read Catherine's nonverbal signals realize that there is more going on in her head than it seems at first. A night aide once noticed that when she apparently anticipated her mother's quarterly visits, she became more alert than she was between those visits. And when a staff person would remind her that her mother would be coming on a given day, Catherine would not resist, as she usually did, the medications that would calm her and make her time with her mother of better quality. We learned that Catherine would be on her very best behavior the entire day of her mother's visit. If only she could speak, what would she tell us about why she acted in different ways when mom came than when she wasn't around?

Catherine does not like spinach, and she makes this clear by turning her face away from her feeding spoon, but she loves pureed carrots and indicates this by opening her mouth for them. She loves to take van rides on warm, sunny afternoons. She wants to go to bed early in the evening and be tucked in like a little baby. Could it be that she remembers when her mother put her to sleep at night many, many years ago? Although Catherine does not talk, she communicates. To those who take the time and have the patience to get to know her well she communicates about the present much better than it first appears she can. But those secrets of the past are hard, if not impossible, to read.

Catherine also likes the times when her friend, a seminary intern chaplain, comes to her group home on Wednesday afternoons. The chaplain brings a small electronic keyboard, and the people sing the old favorite hymns of the church—"Amazing Grace," "The Old Rugged Cross," and "Jesus Loves Even Me." But even though no words come from Catherine's mouth, all who know her best know by her smiles of recognition that she is singing these songs inside. Those who have the ability to read her messages can almost hear her sing,

Through many dangers, toils, and snares,
I have already come;
'Tis grace hath brought me safe thus far,
And grace will lead me home.

Music speaks to Catherine's heart. And when her chaplain reads the Bible story book, Catherine seems even more attentive than usual. Adam and Eve in the garden, Noah and the ark, Abraham and Isaac on the mountaintop with a ram, and Joseph being sold into Egypt by his brothers. "All of them are my favorites. Read them again and again" seems to be her message.

Catherine's mother helped us understand her love for the music and the Bible stories. Mom remembered that when Catherine was much younger her mother and father would go to the Regional Center, they would have a record player and listen to music together. After the hymns, Catherine's dad would read Bible stories to her. "Oh, how she would enjoy sitting on her daddy's lap and listening to the Bible stories," reported mom on one of her visits. Could we be seeing the significance of those words in Proverbs, "Train a child in the way [she] should go, and when [she] is old [she] will not turn from it" (Prov. 22:6).

It was several years ago that Catherine experienced one of the most devastating weeks of her life. Her mother was to visit Catherine in about a week when a telephone call came to the group home from a friend of the family: "Catherine's mother will not be able to visit her next week. She died peacefully yesterday at eighty-five years of age. Her funeral will be in a few days." But with the message came the suggestion not to tell Catherine. The friend believed that Catherine would not know the difference anyway.

The dilemma that the staff, the seminary intern chaplain, and I as her supervisor faced was whether or not to honor this suggestion. To the people who work with Catherine the assumption that she did not know the difference simply was not true. In fact, Catherine had already been giving indications that she was expecting her mother soon. "Were we to tell Catherine or not?" was the question. If so, how would we tell her? How would she receive the news? "Maybe, she wouldn't be able to handle the news. Maybe it wouldn't make a difference to her anyway," we tried to tell ourselves. But we knew better; she would know if we told her. Yes, her mom's death would be difficult for her. But maybe the difficulty that we struggled with was not so much her difficulty as ours in telling her and dealing with the aftermath of the announcement. How were we going to help Catherine grieve when she heard of her mother's death?

We decided to tell her. We believed that she needed to know. However she would react, we would be there for her just as we had been with other friends who experienced the death of a mother. We would attempt to read her messages back to us to determine what next to do. We determined that the seminary intern chaplain had the best relationship with her and that she should tell Catherine about her mother. The music and Bible story book experiences had built a close relationship between them, and the ministry of grace to a grieving Catherine would probably be most healing through familiar songs and Bible passages: "Amazing Grace," "The Old Rugged Cross," "Great Is Thy Faithfulness," "Jesus Loves Even Me," and the story that relates how David wept at the death of his friend Jonathan.

"Catherine, I have news that is really hard for me to tell you. Your mom will not be visiting you next week. Your mom died yesterday. She's in heaven. Do you remember David and his friend Jonathan in our Bible story? David was sad when his friend Jonathan died. We are so sad about your mom's death, too." These messages were spoken and respoken to Catherine. The old hymn favorites were sung and resung. Was anything getting through? It was so hard to tell.

That evening the staff noticed how agitated Catherine was. Playing tapes of Christian music settled her down, but when the tape stopped, she became disturbed again. Maybe it was because we were half anticipating her disturbance, but for those of us who knew Catherine best we thought she was telling us in her own unique way, "Hey, everybody! Please notice that I am crying too. My mom died!"

To treat her with the dignity and respect that we believe she deserved we became very aware that it was not only all right but necessary that Catherine become agitated and let us know how much she missed her mother. Even Jesus grieved deeply over the death of his close friend Lazarus. As painful as grieving is, it is part of the healing process of grace. But we needed to provide the means of grace to help her experience her grief in helpful and healing ways as well. We who were staff members and chaplains verbalized her pain for her when she experienced the waves of agitation that we believed were evidences of her grief. We determined to allow her to tell us in her own way what it was like to miss her mom. We spoke familiar words of Scripture that give permission to grieve and that give comfort in times of grief. We wanted her to know that this was a very difficult time not only for her but also for us. We sang the great hymns of faith that spoke of God's love for her. Our thinking was, if these words of Scripture and these songs were sources of strength and comfort for us when our loved ones died, would they not also be for Catherine?

"Great is Thy faithfulness! Great is Thy faithfulness! Morning by morning new mercies I see; all I have needed Thy hand hath provided—Great is Thy faithfulness, Lord, unto me." None of us were sure what cognitive messages Catherine received from the words of the song or passages of Scripture. But it seemed that her nonverbal messages to us were that the music, the messages, the love, and the care she received helped her through this crisis in her life. She eventually slept more peacefully. She seemed to respond with a greater receptivity to the visits of her chaplain and their time of Scripture and music together. Oh, there are still times when she has evenings of agitation, and we think that at times she still is missing her mother. Some of us wonder how many messages Catherine gives us with her nonverbal language that we never pick up.

To Think About

1. How do you minister to the spiritual needs of those who cannot communicate with you?

2. What are the most effective ways in which others have ministered to you in your losses and pain? How may they be ways in which people with disabilities also experience God's healing grace?

3. What sensitivities have you developed in reading the non-verbal messages of others to you? How can you turn these into ministry opportunities?

Eleven

"Mom nd dad, i can reed nd rite."

May the words of my mouth and the meditation of my heart be pleasing in your sight, O LORD, my Rock and my Redeemer.

Psalm 19:14

Donald had been diagnosed with autism very early in life. As he grew up, the signs of his autism were noticeable to John and Betty, his parents, and to their friends—the compulsive and repetitive motions, the rocking motion of his body, not making eye contact with others, his very alert mind, his inability to express himself clearly. Donald is very lovable and very intelligent, but it is extremely difficult for him to get his message out. Dozens and dozens of times his parents have thought, *If only there were a way to get inside him and help him maximize his God-given potential.*

Donald is not like some individuals with autism who can talk and communicate their basic needs. Others with autism can multiply, divide, add, and subtract extremely large numbers almost instantly and almost always correctly. Still others can play beautiful music on the piano. Autism shows itself in many different ways.

Donald minds his own business without saying a word, and even though his mannerisms seem to indicate otherwise, he knows what is happening around him. Although he is non-verbal, he is able to point at his watch when it is lunch time and let everyone know that the time has come to get the lunch boxes out of the refrigerator and eat. When staff members at his center for autism discuss having an outing in the park, he is the first to get his coat on and go out to the van. He is bright and generally quite cheerful, but he is shy, withdrawn, and hardly noticeable. Yet with his curious and exploratory nature he checks everything out for himself. No proverbial grass grows under Donald's feet!

Until he was around twenty-seven years old Donald lived with his parents. They have learned to communicate very effectively with each other—mom and dad with words and Donald with gestures, grunts, and groans. John and Betty are well aware that Donald has abilities that most people never see, and in spite of his limitations they believe that God has a purpose for him in the same way as God has a purpose for them and their other three children. They determined, even before Donald was a teenager, that even though he was autistic, he would some day leave home and be on his own, much like his two brothers and his sister. So they planned for the day when Donald would be living independent from them. Parents of children who are disabled have a tendency to shelter and protect them, but John and Betty were determined not to let this happen with Donald.

In Michigan, a person with a disability can receive services from the school system until the age of twenty-six. At that age people like Donald are considered adults. John and Betty talked for years about Donald's living independent from them when he became an "adult." Oh, they sometimes worried about his going out on his own. How would he respond to others, especially if they would not be able to develop the non-verbal communication skills that they had learned to use with each other over the years? Would he withdraw even more if he were in a new place? Would people take advantage of him? Would he make friends with others?

They knew that he was able to keep his room neat and clean. He had demonstrated that he was fastidious about being neat. But could he buy groceries? make meals? keep track of his money? take the bus? The list grew longer as the age of twenty-seven approached. Many times John and Betty thought they had made a mistake. But they realized that Donald was deter-mined to be on his own. He was convinced that buying gro-ceries, making meals, keeping track of money, or taking a bus was no big deal. He could and would do it easily.

When the time came, John and Betty worked out an arrangement with Christian Homes for Donald to share an apartment with another person who complemented his person-ality. Christian Homes is a residential program especially designed to enable people like Donald to live in a distinctively Christian, semi-independent home with a support network. Today Donald's parents are very relieved and convinced that this is the home where God wants Donald to live, but they went through some very anxious times as he left home to be on his own. He shares a two-bedroom apartment with Arnold, a person who has Down's syndrome. Arnold isn't very good at keeping his room clean, but he has better cooking skills than Donald, and everyone believes they can complement each other's abilities. A staff person checks up on Donald and Arnold daily and assists them in learning those aspects of inde-pendent living that they still need to master.

Grocery shopping has continued to be a big concern for both Donald and Arnold, especially in the matter of money management. But they are learning to do their own shopping with the help of support staff. Donald quickly discovered how to pay for his food, but Arnold seemed to be better at knowing what foods they needed for meals and snacks. Donald quickly learned to make macaroni and cheese and to fry hamburgers. After several attempts Arnold now knows how to make an edible tuna fish casserole and to bake fish sticks. For the first few months of living together Arnold and Donald baked potatoes in their microwave and ate them for every meal. Now Arnold has learned to make rice for one meal and chicken stuffing out of a box for another. The support staff taught Donald to cook frozen vegetables, which they supplement with baked potatoes. Donald taught Arnold how to keep his room clean, and now Arnold is even more compulsive about having the house clean than Donald with his ritualistic cleanliness. But Arnold taught Donald to put the garbage in trash bags, and together they take their garbage to the road every Monday morning—"the day after church day."

The day that Donald became independent and moved into his apartment with Arnold was a momentous day for both of them and for their families. And it was challenging, especially since Donald could not talk. The limitations of his autism have remained, and the strengths and weaknesses of both his and Arnold's disabilities present unique challenges for them. They have had to learn ways to communicate with each other. They have had to learn to get along with each other. They have learned the skills of daily living without their parents looking over their shoulders. This has not been easy for them. But their parents, likewise, have had to learn to be supportive while backing away and letting their children mature. It has truly been a challenging experience for everyone.

But as significant as was the day that Donald and Arnold moved into the apartment, the day Donald received a type of computer called a facilitator board was even more freeing. The occupational therapist (O.T.) at Donald's sheltered workshop called for a meeting of Donald, John and Betty, Arnold, Arnold's parents, and the lead staff person working with them at the apartment. He raised this issue: Would everyone be willing try an experiment with Donald and Arnold, helping them to communicate through the use of a facilitator board? The device the O.T. suggested was much like a laptop computer, by which Donald could type in words and/or point at pictures on the keyboard. Donald could perhaps let Arnold know what he wanted with this device.

When the facilitator board was opened up for Donald to use in that meeting, he was asked to type something on the keyboard. He quickly went to it, and with the confidence of a typist who knew what he was doing but with the diminished skills of a one-finger technician, he typed, "Mom nd dad, i can reed nd rite. this s goin to hep me tell vrybody what i think bout."

When asked if he could point on his computer to a picture of a bed, Donald touched the picture and the facilitator board announced, "Make your bed." The picture of a happy face announced "I am happy." When Donald experimented with the icon showing a toilet, they all heard "I have to go to the bathroom." Arnold soon got in on the experiment as well. He touched the dishes picture when asked to find the dishes on the board, and the machine blurted out, "Wash dishes."

The liberator opened a whole new way of communication for Donald. Words that could not be spoken by his lips were communicated through his fingers. Donald's life blossomed by his ability to communicate and take more responsibility for himself. The grace of God is like that for all his people. It grows through using our abilities for him. God's grace now flows with a new sense of awesomeness for Donald.

To Think About

1. How important is it to the Christian well-being of everyone to establish a healthy separation between parents and their children with disabilities?
2. What grace-filled significance do you place on your ability to communicate your thoughts and desires to others?
3. How are adaptive devices such as a facilitator board, a wheelchair, and a hearing aid a kind of "means of grace" for those who need them?

Twelve

"What is 'normal' anyway?"

*I always pray with joy because of your partnership
[with me] in the gospel.*

Philippians 1:4–5

I met Pastor Jim Vanderlaan when he applied to serve in a Clinical Pastoral Education (CPE) internship at Pine Rest Christian Mental Hospital. He and the CPE supervisor at Pine Rest thought he might explore serving his internship at Hope Network, in a ministry that serves people with disabilities. He had been a pastor for about twenty years and was not certain what his options would be as he left his church to explore some new kind of service.

Clinical Pastoral Education is an integrative learning process that many pastors and seminary students take as we develop our pastoral ministry skills and work through who we are as God's agents of grace. I say "we" because it is the educational process that I too took part in to enter the chaplaincy. It is a process that focuses on assessing and developing the psychological, social, mental, and spiritual dimensions of oneself and one's ministry while engaging in a pastoral ministry.

What piqued Jim's interest in a CPE internship at Hope Network was the fact that he would be serving persons with disabilities. Jim is blind, and he has never really considered himself handicapped by his disability. Yet he indeed has a disability, one that both limits him and equips him for ministry. Like many other people with disabilities, he has never let his limitation stop him from being and doing whatever he believed God wanted for his life. The challenge of the CPE internship would help him to learn about himself in the context of ministry. But learning how his disability and abilities would be used in ministry to people with whom he would serve as a chaplain would certainly be part of the growth process that he and I would experience together. Certainly a crucial issue raised by Jim's internship was this: What difference is there between serving God as a person who is blind and serving him as one who is—what word can I use here?— one who is "normal"? What is "normal" anyway? Am I "normal"? I am about as "normal" as Jim.

My role in this internship was to be Jim's mentor. Yet in many ways he was my mentor as well. He, as well as I, brought a wealth of experiences that enhanced each other's lives and our ministry together. He had completed his doctorate in Christian ethics before I completed my seminary training. Although I did not have him as a professor, he was teaching courses in ethics and apologetics at the seminary we both attended. He became a pastor in a church setting about the same time I entered the church pastorate. I served in two different church ministries before taking my CPE and entering a chaplaincy ministry with persons who were substance abusers. At the same time Jim served as the pastor of three churches in quite different settings and ministry challenges. His responsibilities of preaching, serving the sacraments, calling on the sick and on other members of the community, teaching church education, and directing the

program of a church were the same kinds of ministry functions
as those I performed. I was a father of three children in college,
high school, and elementary school; he was a father of seven
children from post-college to early elementary school. I served
as a person who was sighted; he, as a person who was blind. I
soon realized that I received my title as mentor only because I
had completed CPE before Jim and had served in chaplaincy
ministries longer than he. So what is "normal" anyway?

The question of what or who is normal was actually raised
very early in our ministry. I'm sure I raised the question more
often than Jim at first. If Jim is blind, then what am I? Sighted?
Yes, but am I really normal? If one of our mutual "parishioners"
has autism or a mental illness or the Prader-Willi syndrome,
then are we "not autistic," "not mentally ill," or "not Prader-
Willi"? Are we called normal and they not normal? We soon
realized that the old paradigms of pigeonholing people do not
make sense, especially because the people we minister to are
real people. In many ways, Jim was miles ahead of me in realizing this, because he did not consider himself disabled, or if he
was disabled, he was sure it didn't matter. Yet he too had to face
these questions squarely with the people he served.

This question of "normality" continued to be worked out
in other ways as well. Jim was assigned to a wide range of ministry sites. Small group homes and big dormitory housing facilities, large factories and small job shops, hotel buildings and
Burger King restaurants are the places where Jim and I find the
people to whom we minister. Our ministry is community
based. In the ministry at Hope Network we go where people
live and work. But Jim is blind; or more politically correct, he
has a sight impairment. Because he has a sight impairment, he
is not able to drive to those places. So my first dilemma was
how he would get to wherever he was to do his ministry? It

wasn't at all Jim's dilemma, of course. I took him to each site for the first time, and he took the Go Bus after that. He knew how to use existing transportation systems.

One of the first days of the internship, I drove Jim in my car to a local manufacturing firm and to a small sheltered workshop in the community. At these sites I introduced Jim to the people he would pastor for the next year. As we passed through certain intersections along the various roads to each site, Jim told me that we had just passed Eastern Avenue and 52nd Street, then Eastern and 44th, and finally Eastern and 36th Street. "Here is where you turn right, isn't it?" Okay, so who is "normal" anyway?

As we walked past the doors of the manufacturing company, Jim started counting the steps that he had to walk before we made a sharp 90-degree left turn. Then he continued counting the paces he made before making a second sharp 90-degree turn, this time to the right. Eventually we walked through a set of doors and into a room 20 degrees to the left and 25 feet straight ahead. I learned that Jim mapped out the places in his life that he would frequent so that he knew how to get where he wanted to be. At the site I introduced him to the job coach and to twelve employees who had experienced head injuries at an earlier time in their lives. Jim talked to each one. He found out what their names were, what jobs they were working on, something pertinent about each person, and the telephone number of the work site so that he would be able to call them if he ever needed to do so. As we walked out, Jim surprised me with the comment, "Well, I know how to find this place now. Where do we go next?" I say, what is normal anyway? Am I maybe working with someone who is "supernormal"?

The stories could go on forever about the experiences of normality that Jim experienced every day. Jim would sometimes walk between the locations of various job-placement sites that were a mile or more apart because the Go Bus shuttle service was slow and unreliable. Even in the wintertime when the sidewalks were covered with snow, he made his way from the side door of one location to the front door of the next place, knowing very well where he had been and where he was going. He led Bible studies with persons who were mentally ill, and he had a "sixth sense" to understand when people were either really hurting or pulling his leg. I still marvel at his developed ability to be aware of things about people that I can learn by being sighted.

In this year of internship Jim was able to develop his ability to lead small group "spiritual growth classes" with persons who typically were reluctant to voice their insights and opinions because of their lack of confidence. I am sure they felt comfortable with him because he was comfortable with his own disability and theirs as well. On weekends he conducted worship services at the Pine Rest Chapel (see chapter 19 to learn about these services). He and his wife (who plays the piano) had cleverly devised a system between them to lead a fluid and challenging worship service with persons who had developmental limitations.

Jim also had his moments when he walked into people and tripped over misplaced items in hallways and on work floors. He would get stuck in an apartment complex where he had set up appointments to minister, only to learn that they didn't show up and his Go Bus wouldn't come for him for three hours. Whenever I had those kinds of experiences—and I had them too—I could get into my car and go to another location. My gift of sight certainly gave me some advantages in ministry over Jim, but his "gift of blindness" provided other advantages in ministry over mine. So maybe the issue in being normal isn't between being "disabled" and being "normal," but in having different abilities and different disabilities as normal children of God.

Throughout that year Rev. Jim Vanderlaan also developed his abilities to adapt to the wide spectrum of needs that people with differing disabilities experience. I had learned that same year that Jim and I and the people we served were different people with different abilities and even different disabilities. But maybe most important, *I had to learn that we were also all normal.* I wonder how God by his grace looks at all of us.

To Think About

1. In terms of who or what is normal, how have you experienced a relationship with someone with a disability?
2. How do you explain the extraordinary gifts and abilities that some people with disabilities have?
3. What kinds of efforts are you making to see yourself in "partnerships in the gospel" with fellow Christians who are disabled?

Thirteen

"I want to eat Jesus bread."

Then the two told . . . how Jesus was recognized by them when he broke the bread.

Luke 24:35

To make a profession that Jesus Christ is one's Savior and Lord can be one of the most thrilling experiences of a person's life. This is especially true when it is born out of a faith that is initiated by the Holy Spirit, developed in the life of felt needs, and surrounded by a community of genuinely caring saints. I have experienced this in my own life, and I have seen this joy in each of my children. But as a chaplain, first with chemically dependent persons and now with people who are disabled, I have also shared this thrill with many of God's "chosen race and royal priesthood" who are on the fringe of the organized church.

One such person was Judy. Judy's witness to God's grace was especially meaningful to the leaders in her church and then with her whole congregation when she came forward to let others know of God's working in her life. She had known for some time that she wanted others to know that she was a Christian, but she didn't think that the people in the church would receive her affirmation of faith. She had shared this faith

commitment often with especially those who knew her best—
her father, mother, her three other sisters, and a small group of
other people with developmental disabilities. She knew that
she loved Jesus, but she didn't know how to say it very well.

Judy has cerebral palsy, and she is mildly retarded. She has
struggled with learning disabilities at school. Her cerebral palsy
has caused a mobility impairment so that she has to walk with
a four-footed walker. She has difficulty speaking clearly, but if
she speaks slowly and if others pay attention, she can be understood. Those who know her well realize what a unique person
she is. Those who do not know her think she is incapable of
acting responsibly, thinking rationally, and speaking clearly.
Amazingly, she lives up to the expectations of each group when
she is in their presence. Her family and close friends see her as a
serious, sensitive, and committed Christian. But most of the
people in her church and many people who have never taken
the time to get to know her think of her as a mumbling and
simpleminded person. What makes this so self-defeating for
Judy and those have not gotten to know her is that they feed
off the fears and prejudices of each other. This creates an even
greater distance between them.

It was this false image of her as an incapable, nonthinking,
and profoundly retarded person that almost got in the way of
one of the most thrilling days in the life of God's people of
whom Judy is a member. With the encouragement of a few
individuals who knew her best, Judy asked to meet with her
church elders to let them know that she wanted to "join the
church." Although none of the church leaders wanted to say no
to her, they wrestled with the question of whether she really
understood the seriousness and the meaning of "professing her
faith" and "joining the church." At first they wanted to delay
her coming before them, but they decided that the pastor

should see her first and examine her knowledge of the Christian faith and tell them what he found.

That decision turned out to be the best decision they could ever have made. Judy's pastor did more than simply assess her faith; he got to know her in a way he had not known her before. He took the time to carefully and patiently listen to her. It was difficult, but he soon realized how simple and profound her faith was. Her enthusiasm for the Lord, the love and genuine caring she demonstrated to her pastor, even the pictures on the wall of her room were all part of a message of a deeply committed faith that he observed and heard in his time with her. He talked to her parents and discovered how sure they were of her faith and how proud they were of her desire to share it at church. He even had the opportunity to meet some of her friends who were disabled much as she was. He discovered the depth of their relationship with each other as Christians.

But it was her understanding of communion and her desire to eat the bread and drink the cup that opened the door for her to the elders and eventually to the whole congregation.

Judy was scared when she thought about going to the Monday evening elders' meeting, but less so after the meetings with her pastor. She knew he was a friend who really cared about her. This relationship of Christian love assisted in communicating a genuine and joyous Christian life in both what she said and how she said it. Like the pastor when he came to her home, the elders had to listen carefully and patiently to her because she was so difficult to understand. When some had a puzzled look on their faces, the pastor would check with Judy about what she said. Together they all "labored" to be understood and to understand—Judy in trying to make herself clearly understandable and the elders in deciphering words from her sometimes mumbling sounds.

Finally, Judy's pastor raised the leading question that he knew was at the heart of her faith. "Judy, why do you want to share your faith with us today and with the whole church next week?"

"I want to eat Jesus bread." Everyone heard her words clearly. "I can't wait until I can eat Jesus bread and drink Jesus juice. People who love Jesus are the ones who eat Jesus bread." There was passion and conviction in Judy's voice as she spoke.

"Tell us what Jesus bread is," asked the pastor, knowing what her answer would be because of his conversations with her at home.

"Jesus' skin and meat turned into bread and Jesus' blood and guts turned into juice—that's Jesus' bread and Jesus' juice, and I want to eat it and drink with all the other Christians at church 'cause I love him so." The thrill and joy of one of God's children heralding her heart's desire was not only heard by the elders but also felt by them. The Holy Spirit seemed to light a spiritual spark from her heart to their hearts, and everyone was blessed.

And the wind and the fire of the Holy Spirit didn't stop in that Monday night elders' meeting. The next Sunday morning was communion Sunday. On the marquee in front of church that Sunday were the words "Come and eat Jesus bread and drink Jesus juice with Judy." In the sermon the pastor told of his meeting with Judy, her parents, and her friends. He was given the words by God to describe the thrill of Judy's testimony of faith in the elders' meeting. Judy was asked to come forward to share her faith with the church before the Lord's Supper was shared. She was again asked, "Judy, why do you want to share your faith with us today?"

Maybe her spontaneously spoken words were not the same as those of the prior Monday evening, but her conviction and clarity of speech were. "I want to eat Jesus bread, and I want to drink Jesus juice, 'cause I love him so much." Her faced beamed. The joy on her face and in her words was contagious. Those who really didn't know Judy very well before now found a point of "oneness in Christ" in the breaking of the bread and the drinking from the cup, not too unlike the two who walked with Jesus on the road to Emmaus and recognized him when he broke bread with them.

The pastor then extended to the congregation a novel but understandable invitation to the table of our Lord. "Come and eat Jesus bread and drink Jesus juice with Judy." You can guess who the first person was at the Lord's table that morning with her beaming, grace-filled face. Certainly Judy shared God's grace with the congregation with her testimony of faith. But most people that morning remembered God's grace as Judy joined them at the communion table and feasted on God's grace with Jesus bread and Jesus juice.

To Think About

1. What barriers are raised by the bureaucracy of churches that prevent persons with disabilities from experiencing the fullness of being members of God's people?

2. What barriers do disabilities themselves erect to prevent these blessings from happening not only for the person with a disability but for the whole church as well?

3. How willing are you to be an advocate for the people in your church who have disabilities so that they too can be vital members who contribute to the total ministry of God's people?

4. Discuss the matter of people's living up (or down) to the expectations placed on them.

Fourteen

"Well done, good and faithful servant": A Tribute to God's Grace

Well done, good and faithful servant! You have been faithful with a few things; I will put you in charge of many things.

Matthew 25:23

Steve Johnson died. This is his real name, and I use it with the permission of his family. His funeral, much like his life, was a tribute to the grace of God in Jesus Christ. Many of the people I have written about in this book are not very widely known. Their lives touch only a few other people around them. This was not so with Steve Johnson. I knew for years that he had touched the lives of many people, but I did not realize how many and to what extent until I attended his funeral.

Steve's sudden stroke had been a surprise to his wife, his parents, and everyone who knew him in the Grand Rapids, Michigan, community. The word had spread rapidly, first that he was in a coma and then that he had died—all in just a couple of days. John called me about Steve's stroke and then about his death. John had known Steve as a businessman who ran a tool and die shop outside of town. I knew him as a member of the board of the Christian agency that I work for. John and I decided to go to the funeral home and meet with Steve's wife, parents, brothers and sisters, and literally hundreds of his close friends. The funeral home was filled with people. We discovered then that Steve had had many friends, but we were even more overwhelmed the next day when we came to the church building where the funeral was held and saw the parking lot filled with cars. It was apparent by the large group of people at the church that many people not only had known Steve Johnson but had been deeply touched by his life.

In some ways I was a bit preoccupied before the funeral service. Earlier Steve's father had asked me to say something at the service about Steve's involvement with people with disabilities. So I looked around to see who was present. In the narthex of the church were many people whom I knew to have a disability or to be associated with those who experienced disabilities. Throughout the sanctuary were people seated in wheelchairs or using other adaptive devices to assist them in their disabilities. I recognized some people who had mental illnesses and others with cerebral palsy, multiple sclerosis, head injuries, seizure disorders, and more. Steve knew their struggles because their struggles were his struggles. He went up against government and agency bureaucracies and championed the cause of the disabled, especially when he believed they were not getting a fair shake in life. He fought against the injustices that people with disabilities so often experience in a society that doesn't even know it perpetrates these wrongs. More than several times, he challenged me to get churches and church leaders to reach out to meet the needs of the kinds of people among whom Jesus spent much of his ministry. Clearly Steve's motivation to help those with disabilities came from a deep love he had for them. He himself was disabled, and he knew how much Jesus loved, accepted, forgave, and served as an advocate for him. He could demonstrate that love no less for others.

Ever since a diving accident when he was seventeen, Steve was a quadriplegic. He could guide his power wheelchair with minimal use of his left hand, but most of his physical movements were done with a joy stick, which he often held in his mouth or at his side where he could get at it quickly. A full-time personal-care attendant assisted him for most of his personal needs. Steve was gifted with a sharp intellect and a keen sense of justice. He could clearly articulate what he believed was right and true, and he tirelessly and courageously gave of himself to others. Make no mistake about it, Steve Johnson let everyone know who his Savior and Lord was and how important a personal relationship to Jesus was in the nitty-gritty of life.

As I waited for the funeral service to begin, I recognized lawyers, businessmen and businesswomen, and health care leaders in the church sanctuary. I saw people who were apparently from Korea and were perhaps friends of Mia, Steve's wife, who was born in Korea. Still other people seated in the pews of the beautiful sanctuary were from Vietnam. Until someone from that community came forward later in the funeral service to speak, I had no idea what connection Steve had with them.

On the platform of the church were five pastors of some of the most well-known evangelical churches in the area, each of whom claimed that Steve had been an inspiration to them as he lived the grace of God in Jesus Christ. Seated in the front row of the church with Mia was her mother, who had come from Korea for the funeral. Next to them were Steve's mother, father, and siblings, who were both grieving his death and celebrating triumphantly his arrival in heaven. Even before the service began, I could see that today was not going to be a day of doom and gloom. Steve's brothers, sisters, and their spouses and children showed both sorrow and victory on their faces because they were confident of where Steve really was at that moment. Sitting near to where John and I sat was a woman who was close to the family but was apparently not a family member. She radiated a warm loving glow too.

What struck me as I sat there was that all these people had stories to tell of their relationship with Steve, and each one was special in his or her own way. I was only one of many who were given the opportunity to speak in the funeral service. But there was a striking similarity in what each of us said. Steve was a child of the King. He lived a victorious life as a Christian. This funeral was a tribute to God's grace in the life of the one we came to mourn—Steve Johnson.

The five pastors on the platform area of the church read Scripture, poems, and testimonies and gave brief messages from the Scripture. Their theme was the same: God blessed all of us with Steve Johnson's life. One of the pastors singled out the woman with the radiant glow of love and thanked her on behalf of all of us for being Steve's personal caregiver for eleven months. Later she herself come forward. Holding back her tears of joy and sorrow, she read a poem that spoke of the Christian joy she received in serving Steve in a very total and intimate way.

Steve's brother and his ten-year-old nephew spoke a few words. The thing that was special for them, they said, was that this loved family member turned his many adversities in life into opportunities for God to work. A Vietnamese woman told how much work Steve had done in helping to bring other Asians into the United States and getting them involved in a Vietnamese Christian church. In fact, a whole small Southeast Asian community was indebted to Steve's ministry with them. A young daughter of this woman played a short piano solo in honor of Steve as part of the funeral service. Another woman from Vietnam came forward to tell how much love and care

Steve was showing to newly arriving Asians by teaching them how to read. It amazed me that one man could serve the Lord in so many ways, especially when he could not walk, move his arms, drive a car, and do the many things I take for granted.

A sharply dressed black man stood up and walked to the microphone in the front of the sanctuary. He introduced himself as the mayor of Kentwood and said he counted it an honor to be a fellow Christian with Steve. He informed us of the many ways in which Steve came to city hall and state governmental bodies to plead for various causes and to act as an advocate for people in whom he believed. The mayor told us that before the election he had asked Steve to run the mayoral election campaign, and he ran the campaign very successfully. A second man followed the mayor to the microphone and introduced himself as the former mayor of Kentwood. Like his successor, he too gave praise to God for Steve as a fellow Christian and honored him as one of God's servants in our community.

The end of the service was devoted to an altar call. The pastors and Steve's family were all convinced that the testimony of God's grace in Steve's life was an invitation for all to commit or recommit themselves to Jesus Christ. Everyone who ever spoke with Steve Johnson knew that his passion was Jesus. What we found out at his funeral was how extensive and how rich this commitment was in serving others and speaking out for righteousness and justice.

When it was my turn to go to the microphone to tell how God used Steve powerfully with people who were disabled, my words were brief. They concluded with words from Scripture that was a theme I heard throughout the funeral. The more I reflect on these words, the more convinced I am that they articulate the best tribute to God's grace in the life of Steve.

"Well done, good and faithful servant, Steve Johnson. Your life and now your death were and are and continue to be a tribute to the grace of God in Jesus Christ."

To Think About

1. What will be said about God's grace in your life at your funeral? What would you want said? What are you doing now that gives a strong witness to Jesus?

2. How do you turn adversities into opportunities for God to work his grace through you in the lives of family, work mates, friends, and those to whom you reach out?

3. How does your attitude shine out in who you are in the Lord and what others remember about you?

4. How does the lordship of Jesus Christ assist you to become an advocate for those whose lives are at the fringe of our society?

Fifteen

"Are you a Christian? I'm one too."

Let your light shine before men, that they may see
your good deeds and praise your Father in heaven.

Matthew 5:16

Dick works for Zondervan Publishing House. One of the books they publish is *Parables of Hope,* and it is very likely that Dick put the bar code on your book or packed the thirty books bearing this title in the box used to ship your book to the store where you made your purchase. Dick rarely misses a day of work and does his job without many mistakes. He is good at what he does, and he will tell you so if you ask him. He loves working for Zondervan. He often seeks new friends in the cafeteria at his morning or afternoon breaks or at lunch time. It doesn't matter to him whether he is talking to the president of Zondervan, one of the editors, or the forklift driver who picks up the skids of books that he and his friends have packaged. Dick loves to talk with them. He loves people. He loves life. And he loves his God. Anyone at Zondervan who has ever talked with Dick knows that he has a spontaneity about him that brings a surprise to most conversations. So they are often eager and willing to talk with him when he drops in at their table during break times.

My ministry takes me into the work sites where persons with disabilities serve in the community as well as in sheltered workshops. Dick worked in various sheltered workshops, where he demonstrated that he could take on more complex and more responsible work. When a job coach told him about the opportunity to work at Zondervan, he found it hard to express his joy. Zondervan is one of the more sought-after enclaves in the Hope Network system. An enclave is a workforce of approximately twelve to twenty people with disabilities working in an industrial setting and led by a job coach. It is one of the last phases of work training in the Hope Network work training system before one enters competitive employment.

The word out about Zondervan in Dick's informal network of peers is that the working conditions are fantastic at Zondervan. There are windows through which one can look outside, a cafeteria with good food, a great job coach, a place where one can make good money, and fellow employees who really like people with disabilities. For Dick and for some of the other Hope Network employees, one additional factor is also very important: Dick will be the first to tell anyone who asks, "It is a Christian organization, and you can tell the difference." When I come to the front desk at Zondervan for my monthly visit, the secretaries know even before I sign the log that I will be seeing Fred, the job coach, and the Hope people out in the warehouse. I know that Dick and his friends make a special point of greeting the secretaries and anyone they meet as they come in to work in the morning. My visitor's pass may be helpful to some Zondervan employees to identify who I am as I walk to the back part of the building to do my ministry, but most employees know who Dick and his friends are and how to direct me to them.

Coming to their area is a lot like coming into any other department in a warehouse, except that it is immediately evident that the work crew has a variety of disabilities (or differing abilities, depending on what one chooses to emphasize). One person works in a wheelchair. Another person cannot use his right arm. A third person hears with the assistance of a hearing aid. Only in talking with each one personally does one realize that they are developmentally disabled, mentally ill, and/or physically challenged. Dick is one of the first to see me coming. "He's back. Al's here, Randy. The chaplain's here, Joanne. Hey, Fred, Reverend Al's here." The word goes out quickly. I recognize the immediate acceptance and love that come from this crew. The other Zondervan employees have come to experience and appreciate this love at breaks and lunch times every day. It is what makes going to work with this crew as much a ministry to me as mine is to them.

I generally spend a few minutes with each person to find out what has been happening in their lives that week and maybe discover a special ministry need. Sometimes someone has a parent or roommate who has just had surgery, and I am asked to pray for that person. At other times the person I am talking with has waited for me to come so that we can talk about an interpersonal problem that he or she may have with another person. I never know from one visit to the next what the issues will be that a person may want to share with me. Most often, however, I am aware that my ministry is mostly one of what I call "Christ's presence." I represent to Dick and his friends the God we all serve. Just as Jesus often had compassion with the people of his day, the compassion I have with Dick and his friends is a mutual caring in Christ's name that leaves us all with the unspoken affirmation that Jesus has been present and that he cares for us.

As I talk to Dick this morning, he is building display boxes for the Zondervan Family Book Stores so that you may be attracted to books like the one you are reading. The colorful and well-constructed cardboard box display that Dick is working on is a bit complex, but Dick has learned which flaps of the cardboard box need to be folded back and which ones need to be folded to the right and which to the left. When he completes building the box, he puts it on the conveyer belt to Sandra who puts four books in the top section of the display with four different books in the second section and another four books in the bottom section. Randy then takes the display with the books and puts them all in another box that he has assembled and tapes the box for shipping. Steve puts the shipping label on the box, takes this box and other boxes of displays that several other teams have completed, and places them on the skid that is then sent to the shipping department. Each individual and the team take pride in their ability to do good work at their jobs.

As Dick builds yet another display box, he turns rather abruptly to me. "Reverend Al, are you a Christian?" The question startles me for a second because he obviously knows that I am a chaplain. I would have thought that from the other conversations we have had, Dick would have known that I am a Christian. I can't imagine that Dick is trying to test me, but I don't know what is motivating him with the question. "Yes, I am a Christian, Dick. Why do you ask?" is the most direct response I can come up with at the spur of the moment. I generally am not at a loss for words, but this time Dick catches me by surprise.

"Well, I'm one too," he chimes back with a broad smile on his face. "Isn't it great to be a Christian? I only wish that everyone was a Christian. I think being a Christian is simply great. I like asking people if they are a Christian. It makes them think. Some people don't know what to say when I ask them. But I think it's so great to be a Christian that I want everybody to know Jesus." There is a sparkle in his eye, a vitality in his voice, and a genuineness and spontaneity that only Dick in his grace-filled way can display.

I do not remember what exchange of words we had right after that, but I do remember the gist of our conversation. We talked together about the blessings of being a Christian in much the same way that I bask in and enjoy the first bright sunny day after thirty or so dreary days of clouds in the winter. I felt uplifted that day, a little like Peter and John must have felt when they were on the Mount of Transfiguration. As a chaplain, I am supposed to be ministering to Dick and his friends, but that day Dick was ministering to me.

I suspect that at some of those coffee breaks with other new friends some one or two or more Zondervan employees have been asked, "Are you a Christian?" Maybe some people have been taken aback by Dick's question, but I suspect that others have picked up on the joy and vitality of his faith as he got them going in talking about faith together. Certainly Dick is not afraid to obey Jesus' command in Matthew 5:16: "Let your light shine before men, that they may see your good deeds and praise your Father in heaven."

To Think About

1. How spontaneous and genuine is your expression of praise to God with other people so that they respond in giving praise to God quite naturally?
2. In what ways do people like Dick surpass the rest of us in their ability to show love and honesty?
3. Can you think of a time when another person and you had one of those mountain-top experiences with God? What triggered it for you? What did you learn from it?
4. How can you show an attitude of sparkling radiance for Christ to others?

Sixteen

> ## "I watch how you and everyone else worship, and that's how I do it."

Follow my example, as I follow the example of Christ.
1 Corinthians 11:1

Be imitators of God, therefore, as dearly loved children and live a life of love, just as Christ loved us.
Ephesians 5:1–2a

I took Melanie to church because it was our family's responsibility this week to pick her up from the group home and take her to church with us. Melanie used to come to church with her father every Sunday morning, but her father died a number of years ago. I remember that her mother rarely had come to church because she had both physical difficulties and a mental illness. She felt very uncomfortable about leaving home and especially going to church worship services. Eventually Melanie's father had to make the difficult decision of putting his wife in a nursing home. She died not long after her husband died.

Because Melanie's parents had many needs of their own, they had made a decision when she was very young to send her to a Christian adult-care home. Today she and everyone considers this to be her home. Melanie is mildly retarded and is able to function quite well on her own. She is responsible for keeping her own room clean and for sharing in the scheduled times of making meals, cleaning the table, washing the dishes, doing her laundry, and doing whatever chores need doing throughout her home. Melanie works at a supported employment job site where she puts automobile parts on a rack to be painted with Teflon coating. The owner of her company recently received an award from the Grand Rapids Chamber of Commerce for his innovative use of persons with disabilities in his factory. Melanie was proud to be a part of the reason he received his award.

Melanie does not always come to the church I attend, the one in which she was raised. She lives far enough away from church that it is difficult for our members to pick her up for morning worship. But she loves to come to church. Any telephone call I have ever made to her almost always has two requests: "When are you going to have coffee with me?" and "Can you pick me up for church? I want to go to church this Sunday."

On the Sundays that our members do not pick her up, Melanie seems to find a way to attend the Pine Rest chapel near her group home. (I write about this unique worship service in chapter 19.) So I sometimes rationalize to myself that maybe we do not have to pick her up every week. Besides we are busy people. But if the truth were known, nothing is more meaningful to Melanie than to worship with "her people at her church" on Sunday mornings. "Sunday evenings are better at the chapel," she would likely report if she were asked.

As I drive up to her group home, I see her face in her bedroom window. Her hand is vigorously waving to me in recognition of my arrival; her face is beaming with a huge smile. I am told by her care attendants that Melanie is shouting through the house that I have arrived. "Al is here. Reverend Al is here. I'm going to church now. I got to get my coat on. Where are my peppermints? I got to make sure I bring my money for the collection. Al is here. I don't want to be late for church. Goody! Goody! He's here to pick me up. Bye! Goodbye everybody! I'm going to church now."

Even as I come to the door to escort her to my car, she is still putting her arms in her overcoat as she rushes out and makes her way to my car. I can hardly get my greetings out before she starts to talk . . . and talk . . . and talk.

"Drive faster. We don't want to be late for church. I bought a new Sunday dress with Cynthia." "Who is Cynthia?" I can barely get the words out as her conversation continues non-stop. Cynthia is her care attendant. She had gone shopping with Cynthia on Saturday and had purchased the dress with money from her job at the factory. "The house dog died. Susan [her roommate, I learn] is sick with the flu. I really like it that I can go to church today. Thank you for coming and picking me up. Can you come some time next week and take me to McDonald's for a cup of coffee?" It seems as if her conversation was one continuous sentence.

As I am listening with a touch of boredom, I realize how important it is for Melanie to share with me, her fellow church member, every detail of her life that week. *Isn't that what Christian friends do with each other?* must have been her unthought premise behind her flow of words. She doesn't get a lot of opportunities to be with her church friends, and she is bound and determined to make the most of it.

Now and then she catches herself and realizes that she has been doing all the talking. I can almost hear the instructions someone in a socialization class taught her as she asked me, "How are you this Sunday? How are your wife and kids? Are they going to sit with us in church when we get there? Do you think your wife might come sometime and take me out for a cup of coffee too? I like to drink coffee." All the ingredients of friendships I have with others are there, but they are packaged in a way that only Melanie can have with me. I know some people get upset with her nonstop talking and are therefore reluctant to pick her up for church. But I see it as an opportunity for Melanie to fellowship with a fellow Christian though she does it without the social grace that is most helpful in a relationship. The more I think of it, the more I see it as part of my Christian responsibility to help Melanie learn this socialization process. Isn't that what fellow Christians do for one another?

When we arrive at church, all Melanie's chatter turns to silence and reverence. I am sure that most people who do not know her would never realize what she is like, because she never says much at church. She looks like any forty-year-old single female member of the church. Now, I happen to know that Melanie cannot read or write, and yet, as soon as she is in the church building, she goes to the bulletin rack and gets a bulletin to follow along for the service. When we respond to the pastor with the opening sentences from the first page of the bulletin, Melanie is on the first page and her lips are moving and often echoing the last words of a line. And when the lines of the liturgy reflect phrases she recognizes, she speaks right along with the rest of the congregation. Phrases like "for thine is the kingdom and the power and the glory for ever. Amen" and "to the praise and glory of God" and (in response to "The Lord be with you") "And also with you" flow from Melanie's mouth in perfect synchronization with the whole church body.

On this particular Sunday we use music and words that comes both from our church song books and from printed music in the bulletin. As I look over at Melanie, she is singing both old familiar and contemporary songs right along with the congregation (or at least her lips were moving with ours). When we sing from the church hymnal, her hymnal is out.

Sometimes it is upside down, and it is never on the right page. And when we are singing from the printed words in the bulletin, the bulletin is opened to the right page and Melanie's lips are moving.

When the congregation is in prayer, Melanie is praying. When we are listening to the choir as they lift their voices in praise to the Lord, she is attentively engaged in the same act of praise. Only once in that service did I see her slip up. Normally, the offering in our service is given right after the congregational prayer. This time it was not. The pastor placed the offering after the sermon instead of after the prayer. So while we are praying the congregational prayer, Melanie is thumbing through her purse for the money she had set aside for the Lord that week. When the final "Amen" of the congregational prayer is spoken, she is ready to put her money in the offering plate, only to discover that we are about to stand up and sing another hymn. But she quickly recovers and stands up to sing with the body of Christians.

By the time we are listening to the sermon on this Sunday, I have obviously become interested in Melanie and her worship of God. Our pastor often tells a story or a humorous anecdote in the sermon that brings an emotional reaction from the congregation. Our response may be anything from a slight smile to downright laughter. Like many of us, Melanie may do her daydreaming during the sermon, but she never seems to miss the appropriate smile, or snicker, or even laughter in the message.

Melanie is worshiping God with more awareness and attention to what is spoken and what is done in this service than most of us (certainly this is true of me, this time at least). On the way home I ask Melanie how she liked the service and the sermon. "I loved it. I especially like the story about . . ." (and she tells the story we had all laughed about).

I then ask her how she did so well with the liturgy and the songs in the worship. Her answer is really the secret of her worship of God. She replies, "I watch how you and everyone else worship, and that's how I do it." Here I am, watching her while she is watching me and everyone around us. She is extremely alert to hear and see what is happening during worship so that she can be responsive in a similar fashion herself. I am sure that no one realizes what is happening with Melanie unless they watch her as closely as I did today.

An Afterthought

Later I thought about the lesson that Melanie taught me in that Sunday morning worship service, and I began to realize that her way of learning to worship the Lord was not different from my way of learning to worship God. How did I learn how to praise God in the sanctuary but by watching my parents, other adults, and children in the week-to-week time I spent in God's house? I have taught my children too about prayer and Bible study by modeling the outward expressions of my faith. Could that kind of following each other's example and imitating one another (and ultimately Jesus Christ himself) not be the most effective way of sharing our witness to Jesus with each other? Could it not also be that what was happening in our conversation both to and from church was part of the same process of learning what it means to be "members of one another in the body of Christ"?

To Think About

1. Where did you learn the particular expressions of your life in the Lord?

2. How do you go beyond the routine, legalistic expression of faith into a heartfelt and attentive expression of worship and praise?

3. If indeed others are imitating our expressions of faith, how does that change what we want to model to our children and others?

4. How may we assist others like Melanie not just to "do it right" but to experience the fullness of Christ together?

Seventeen

"I don't like hearing. I want to sign and read lips. But what does the Lord want?"

When Jesus saw him lying there and learned that he had been in this condition for a long time, he asked him, "Do you want to get well?"

John 5:6

His parents did not realize it at first, but Gary was born with a hearing impairment. He cooed like other babies, smiled when his parents tickled him under the chin, wet his diapers, and did all the wonderful and amazing things babies do to make their parents burst with pride. There was no doubt about the fact that his parents were proud of him. Because he could hear some sounds and responded to them much as other babies do, it was difficult to detect that he had a hearing problem. But in one of his early physical examinations the doctor became suspicious that his hearing was not quite right. More extensive testing confirmed those suspicions.

Needless to say, Gary's parents were shocked when the doctor gave them the news. They shed many tears over the anticipated losses their darling little baby would experience. But they decided to do what they could to help him. They sought the opinions of several professionals about what could be done to correct his hearing. The best opinion of the experts was that reconstructive surgery could possibly be done on at least one of his ears. There were no guarantees that Gary would hear, but the fact that he could respond to sounds made surgery feasible. The best resources suggested that this surgery be done at a time when he reached mature physical development. It was not wise to do this kind of surgery on a little baby.

Days turned into weeks and years, and Gary's ear surgery kept getting postponed until a later date. In the meantime Gary continued to grow up. Throughout the process, his parents had to make other decisions about what was best for him. He needed to learn communication skills. In the field of hearing impairment a debate goes on as to whether a person should learn sign language, read lips, or do both. Gary's parents decided that he should learn to do both. They reasoned that because he had minimal hearing, his attention could be gained by someone making some kind of noise. Certainly he could communicate best with other people who know "signing," but not all people can sign. Persons who lip-read don't always catch everything that is spoken, but they get along better with persons who cannot sign and who make an effort to face the person who is hearing impaired and engage that person in conversation. Having the ability to do both was best, for obvious reasons, but it required that Gary learn to do both. He actually has learned both systems well. But this decision included the determination that his parents and their other two children learn sign language as well if they were to communicate effectively with him.

When it was time for Gary to go to school, other decisions had to be made. Should he go to a school for the deaf or should he go to a regular school? They decided to have him go to a regular school. If he had been born ten or fifteen years earlier, going to a school for the hearing impaired would have been their only option. But now inclusion of persons with disabilities in the school system was possible, and they decided to have Gary start school in a regular public school. They looked for and found a school that had the support systems to help him when he faced difficulties.

Gary did well at school academically. Perhaps this was because he had caught on to reading lips so well as a preschooler. His accomplishments in elementary school work were aided by teachers who could sign. They helped him with learning to read lips and encouraged him to write his messages when he needed help. He faced difficulties with his classmates at first. Some of the children seemed to pick on him because they saw him as different. This could have caused continuing difficulties had not one of the teachers intervened with the kids that were picking on him. She helped them to see life from his point of view. Most of his friends knew that he had a hearing impairment. They soon learned that they had to tap him on the shoulder to get his attention and make sure that he was looking at them when they wanted to talk. Occasionally, they or Gary, and sometimes both, were embarrassed that he did not know details that his classmates had heard in class. They often assumed that he could hear.

Gary had gone to doctors all his life to find help for his hearing. The specialists in his hometown all knew him. Experts at the university hospitals had consulted with his doctor on numerous occasions. Differences of opinions arose about whether he would ever have his hearing restored. Hearing aids were tried, but with little success. In the meantime, Gary finished elementary school and eventually completed high school. He did well at school. His hearing impairment did not stop him from running on the fall cross-country teams and the spring track teams. He seemed to know when the starting guns for races were fired. He certainly knew where the finish lines were, and he ran with hundreds of other runners who had no idea that he had a disability. He was no superstar, but he enjoyed being part of the team with the rest of his schoolmates.

Gary studied computers in high school, and by the time he started college he knew that he wanted to be an engineer. With a clear focus on his career goals and with all the adaptations he had learned, he was able to compensate for his hearing impairment. He was fully as successful at college as he was in his earlier educational efforts. Computers put him on a common ground with other students and provided a written communication form by which he could even "converse" better than most of his colleagues.

Although Gary had not dated much before going to college, he started dating in college. Most girls did not realize that he was deaf until they started to date him. The nasal tone of voice that many deaf people have was not very noticeable in him. The fact that he rarely ever conversed with young women on the telephone did not strike most of them as being all that unusual. On some of his first dates it took a while for a young woman to realize that he understood her only when he was looking directly at her to read her lips. Some second dates never took place because his impairment was unsettling to a few of the women. But for the most part, Gary had only minimal difficulties because of his hearing deficiency.

Gary accepted Jesus as his Savior and grew in his faith life much as he accepted and grew with his disability. The Lord was always real and always important to him. He turned to the Lord for help with all of his challenges. Sometimes he took the Lord for granted in his life; at other times he absolutely could not go one step forward without the Lord directing his faith. When he openly declared his faith in Jesus Christ, it was very natural for him to say that he could hardly remember a time when he did not believe that God's grace enfolded his life.

One of the greatest challenges in his faith and in his relationship to the Lord came after he had completed an undergraduate degree in engineering and started a new job with an engineering firm. A trip to a new doctor revealed a new possibility that his parents had been praying for since his birth. A new surgical technique had been perfected so that his hearing in one ear could possibly be restored up to 100 percent. If it worked, it was possible to attempt to correct his hearing in the second ear as well.

Gary had lived his whole life up to this point hearing only minimal sounds. Now he had the possibility of hearing 100 percent. He had come to accept a world and others in this world, a life and career, relationships to other people—all basically without sound. The first thought he had was *Terrific! Great! Let's go for it!* But it wasn't long before another thought horrified him: *Do I really want this? How will I live with distracting noises around me? I don't like hearing. I want to sign and read lips. But what does the Lord want?*

To those of us who experience sound and sight as a common part of life's experience Gary's dilemma would be comparable to facing the choice of having our hearing or our sight taken away. Would we want that? Of course not; but his question had faith overtones when he asked the deeper question of what God would want of him. Certainly his life had been blessed by the Lord maybe even *because* he had a disability. What if the disability were to be removed? Hearing sometimes creates great difficulties for people who hear. What greater difficulties would it cause someone who doesn't hear?

After praying about it, Gary decided to have the corrective surgery. But after the surgery his hearing improved only 25 percent. Then, after more prayer, he decided not to have any more surgery done. He had learned to live a full and meaningful Christian life without hearing. Hearing was not that important to him anymore.

To Think About

1. If you were to have to make the decision that Gary did, what would you decide? Why?
2. Why are we not strongly aware of grace when life goes on amazingly well day after day? Are we not experiencing God's grace all the time?
3. How are events like Gary's major decision to get surgery on his ear crucial faith-building and grace-experiencing times in our lives?
4. How are these major decision-making times different from and in what way are they the same as the many thousands of other decisions that we have to make?

Eighteen

"I lost 182 pounds. It's work, but with God's help I'm doing it."

I can to everything through him who gives me strength.

Philippians 4:13

Dennis has that rare disability called the Prader-Willi syndrome. Although his parents did not recognize the syndrome early in his life, his insatiable appetite and poor sucking abilities were clear indicators of the Prader-Willi disability. All of his life, Dennis had the problem of putting on too much weight. Some of us have problems with being heavy because of a combination of genetics and learned unhealthy eating patterns. I certainly do, especially when I see obesity in my parents and grandparents on both sides of my family. When I look at my eating behavior with fatty foods and calorie-laden treats, I see addiction issues with food that have both genetic and learned behavior overtones. Dennis's Prader-Willi syndrome may look like the same obesity issue that I and many other people struggle with, but it isn't.

Prader-Willi is unique. The body chemistry is such that whenever Dennis eats more than 1,400 calories, he puts on weight. He is continuously hungry. He has no "turn off" system in his body to tell him when he is full. Any piece of food left out in his house or in public is food that he craves and may very well sneak. If left unattended, he may eat gum found on the street or the leftover communion bread at church. Although most people with Prader-Willi experience various degrees of mental retardation, Dennis has an average intelligence—but one of the characteristics of the syndrome is that one's intellectual abilities will decrease. He is unusually short and has a curvature of the spine called scoliosis, characteristics that are also common with the syndrome. His hands are unusually small, and he has hormonal and digestive-system abnormalities. Because he is always hungry, food is always on his mind, and he is easily irritated. I just described Dennis's disability, but I have not described who Dennis is.

Dennis is one of God's children. "I am one of God's kids," he once said. Although he struggles with body chemistry and eating difficulties in ways most of us cannot imagine, he does so as a Christian, redeemed by Jesus Christ. He lives in a community of people who also have the Prader-Willi syndrome, and everyone in his community shares a common Christian faith. Staff members are available to assist Dennis and his friends with their insatiable urge to eat and the other problems associated with their affliction. Dennis prepares his calorie-regulated meals but with supervision so that he will not sneak food. All outings to restaurants, grocery stores, clothing stores, and even a movie are accompanied by a staff person to ensure that no one will sneak extra food. The craving of these people is so strong that any one of them could go on a binge and put on ten to fifteen pounds in a day and then tell stories to cover up what they have done. All food is kept in locked cupboards, refrigerators, and freezers. The battle against wanting to eat all the time is a day-in-and-day-out phenomenon that does not let up for Dennis and his friends.

A typical day for Dennis starts at 7:00 A.M. He eats a breakfast that he has prepared the evening before with a staff person. Sometimes he exercises before taking a Go Bus to a supported work site. At his workplace people have been alerted to his propensity to pilfer food out of other people's lunches. Because he is a good worker, at one time Dennis and the professionals who work with him decided that he would take a job answering telephones at a nursing home near his home. He did the job well, but each day he came home heavier because the nursing and cafeteria staff left food lying around. Dennis could not resist eating the snacks that were left out. No one saw him eating the food, but the truth became obvious when he returned home to his daily weigh-in. Eventually he had to give up his job. Undoubtedly he will continue to work for the rest of his working career at a supported employment site where his eating patterns can be monitored. Dennis works until 4:00 each day under the watchful eye of others to prevent him from eating before taking a Go Bus home again.

When Dennis arrives at home each evening, he carefully schedules his next two hours. A twenty-minute walk with the dog; then thirty minutes on exercise equipment. When he completes his exercise, it is time to make all his meals for the next twenty-four hours. Food is taken from locked pantries for tomorrow's breakfast, for a bag lunch to eat at work, and for his evening meal. It has been only recently that Dennis makes his own meals. He has demonstrated that he can do his own cooking, but a staff person still monitors the process so that he will not eat anything more than what his diet requires. Dennis sets time aside right after dinner for personal devotions.

As I said, Dennis and his friends occasionally go to restaurants and to the movies. Wherever they go, a definite plan for food intake is followed. The menu from the restaurant to which they may go is carefully studied at home before they leave. The meal is carefully selected from a "health smart" list. Calories and fat grams are scrupulously calculated. If the chef at the restaurant slips up and a meal that is not ordered comes through, the staff person accompanying him makes sure that the meal is returned and the right order is received. Popcorn or candy at the movies is not allowed, nor calorie-laden snacks between meals. When Dennis attends a church potluck, he is allowed to eat only the food that he brings from home. Needless to say, he is often discouraged with the preoccupation everyone has with food in his life.

After dinner and devotions, Dennis is responsible for cleaning up whatever mess he has made in the preparation of his three meals. He religiously watches the news on television. Throughout the rest of the evening, he watches selected programs on television or reads mystery novels. One of the characteristic habits of people with Prader-Willi syndrome is to pick at their fingernails and skin until they start to bleed. Whenever Dennis consciously attempts to avoid this annoying behavior, he is successful. But if he watches television or reads a book and stops thinking about the picking behavior, he very well might pick at his fingernails until they are bleeding again.

Dennis is well-read about his Prader-Willi disorder. He can clearly articulate the struggles, the challenges, and the complications of his disability. Many of his friends with Prader-Willi experience a lot of denial about their disability. They don't think they have a problem with food, the problem is not really that bad, or they can manage to eat properly now. Dennis accepts his disability somewhat better than the others, but he still faces an insatiable craving for food. Sometimes he wakes up at 4:00 in the morning feeling totally famished. He once told us that a guest came to his home after eating at Pizza Hut. For the whole time that the guest was in the home, Dennis smelled the pizza on his clothes and all he could think about was *I want a pizza.*

"Having the Prader-Willi syndrome is not easy," Dennis once told me. "I'm hungry all the time. I have a bunch of physical problems that are associated with this disability. I get irritable a lot. I don't like it that the staff has to dog me all the time, but I know that they have to do it or I could weigh up to 400 or 500 pounds. But you know, I lost 182 pounds. It's work, but with God's help I'm doing it. Not perfectly. Not always with the right attitude. But I am doing it."

I can relate to Dennis's Prader-Willi syndrome because of what I know to be my food addiction. His testimony of God's grace in the middle of one lifelong struggle with food is one I want to remember to help me in my eating behavior.

To Think About

1. In what ways do you identify with Dennis and the Prader-Willi syndrome? How does God's grace aid you in your ongoing struggles?

2. How can each of us be part of the resolution of other people's difficulties rather than contribute to them by the excess food we put before them?

3. How do you experience God's strength in your addictions and trials?

Nineteen

"We worship here 'in spirit and truth.'"

God is spirit, and his worshipers must worship in spirit and in truth.

John 4:24

I have just returned from leading the morning worship at Pine Rest Chapel, where some of the people in the Grand Rapids area who have disabilities worship on Sunday. I have been thoroughly blessed by the worship of God's people, most of whom have mental impairments and mental illnesses. Worship at the chapel is spontaneous, it is from the heart, and it is expressed with joy and simplicity. I do not experience in most church worship services what I treasure in the praise of the Lord with and by God's people at the chapel. It is worship "in spirit and in truth" in the fullest sense. As such, it is unique and powerful. I only wish you could be there to sense how real and meaningful it is. But let me try to tell you what the blowing of the wind of the Holy Spirit in our worship meant this morning.

I arrived about fifteen minutes early. As at most services, there were things that needed to be done before the service began: open the doors, set up the microphone, turn the lights on, get the bulletins in the racks, and meet the people as they come into the building. However, as I came to the front door this morning, Marcus was outside waiting for me. He was eager to shake my hand, and he asked if he could sing a solo in this morning's time of worship. He had been practicing "Amazing Grace" in his group home for two hours before coming to chapel. So he was prepared to praise God. I believe that he was led by the Holy Spirit to be our special music today. I gladly gave him permission to sing after the offering and before the sermon.

Soon other worshipers arrived on foot, in wheelchairs, with a tricycle, and in several vans. Greeting God's worshipers as they arrive at the chapel is always a treat for me. Robert greeted me by pointing to his shoes. He was wearing new shoes to church today, or were they really new? They were new several months ago when I led worship at the chapel.

Edgar walked into the chapel arm-in-arm with Esther. They have been boyfriend and girlfriend for years. She carried his quarter for the offering to the front of the sanctuary and carefully placed it in the offering plate before sitting down. "Edgar, I put your quarter in the collection, dear." Edgar, on the other hand, realized that I was the pastor for today after he sat down in his front row seat. I could almost read his mind: *My "regular chaplain" is on vacation today. I need to welcome Reverend Al to lead worship.*

"Reverend Al, it's good to have you back in chapel," he told me with the slow drawl of a speech pattern that I recognized as resulting from heavy medication. "I remember when you were in seminary and we used to rake leaves together. Let's see, that was in August 1965."

Edgar remembers much better than I the details of my summer job at Pine Rest thirty years ago when I was in seminary and he was a young teenager at Children's Retreat, which was the unit at Pine Rest Christian Mental Hospital for children who were developmentally disabled and those who were mentally ill. It is closed now because of the deinstitutionalization of state and private mental hospitals. (For many years individuals with disabilities were sent to state and private mental hospitals and regional centers. Their lives were strictly regimented because they lived in mass dormitories and huge institutions. But since the late 1960s, these people have been returning to the communities in which they were born and where many still have family members.)

Although many such people are now attending worship services with their families, the Pine Rest Chapel is a favorite place for them to worship. The services there are focused on the unique needs and desires of individuals who gather to praise God.

It wasn't long before people were coming through every door of the chapel. Some of the very lowest-functioning persons with mental impairments were escorted by staff persons who assist them when they are out in society. Five or six people came from the "house with many rooms" for persons with mental illnesses (see chapter 21) across the street from the chapel. Three members of the Tuesday afternoon Bible study group (see chapter 7) arrived through the front door of the chapel directly opposite from me. Many waved affirming greetings to me and reached out to fellow Christians with whom they have worshiped at the chapel for years. Everyone who comes to worship picks up a bulletin at the chapel door, even though most in the room cannot read or write. They hold and study their bulletins in such a way that seems to indicate that there is a great deal of news about their church community and the liturgy, for the service is complex. In reality, there was no news in this week's bulletin, and the order of worship was both simple and the same as it has been for many years. Only my

Scripture text, sermon title, and song numbers were different from those listed in last week's bulletin.

Larry pushed his friend Joan in her wheelchair through the back door of the chapel where the ramp is located. On Joan's lap was Larry's guitar. Larry has appointed himself to be the music leader of the chapel. He can only strum his guitar. He knows nothing about chords or rhythm. But he can and does strum every song we sing whether he knows the song or not. And we sing at his pace—slow, very slow and meditative. Joan is so proud of Larry. Always when he finishes during the early singing, she invites him to sit next to her, and they hold hands throughout the rest of the service.

I raised my hands to extend the Lord's greeting to his people. "The grace of the Lord be with you in Jesus Christ." Around the room were a handful of worshipers with their hands lifted with the same blessing I extended, only more eloquently spoken: "Hi-ya, Al. God bless you, Al. Glad you are here today. Good to see you again. Blessings!"

"Let's worship God now!" I invited his people. "Sing number 484" is the response I heard from the third row. Number 484 is the song number Bill always requests in every service. I know it is one of the only two songs he knows by heart. Then I said, "Some other time we will sing 484, but today we are singing number 397, "They will know that we are Christians by our love." "Ya, that's okay; I know that one too," Bill chimed back. Today I played my accordion as an accompaniment to Larry, our guitarist. Sometimes we have guest piano players who accompany him, but today I had the responsibility. Together, we led God's people, who sang a very loud and heartfelt monotone rendition of "They will know that we are Christians by our love." I really believe that God smiled as we sang our hearts out in the chapel under the musical leadership of Larry and me. I suspect that God listens in much the same way I remember listening with glee to my children when they were three, four, or five years old singing their songs of praise at the annual Sunday school Christmas programs.

When it was time for the "congregational prayer" this morning, it truly was a prayer of the congregation that was offered. Fifteen to twenty people came to the front of the sanctuary to lead the prayer. The microphone is a very important aid in our prayer. Each person who took his or her turn to talk to God did so by talking into the microphone, and when they had finished, they handed the microphone to the next person. Even some who have the most difficulty in speaking came forward to offer intercession and praise to God. With a finger pointing at people around the room, Sue Ann prayed, "And da, and da, and da, and da, and da, and da, and da, and da . . . and da. Amen." I knew that she was praying for personal needs. Peter's words were more quiet. They were very difficult for us humans to understand, but God knew very well the words he uttered, words that I thought I understood as ". . . my mom and my dad . . . house mom and house dad . . . be a good boy . . . have a good day. Amen."

Gloria, on the other hand, was much more articulate as she too prayed, "God, be with Reverend Al as he preaches. Help him to speak good so that we can understand him. And be with my mom as she is in the nursing home. Help Sally's mom there too [pointing to Sally in the fifth row from the back]. Forgive me when I'm bad to my staff caregiver. God, tell Frank to say that he's sorry too for having a temper tantrum in the home. Thank you, Jesus, for forgiving my sin. All this I pray in Jesus' name. Amen."

The offering followed the prayer. Eight or ten would-be deacons scrambled out of their seats to literally "lift the offer-

ing." Any effort on my part to select three "collectors" was
ruled out by the "first come, first take the offering" rule of the
chapel. The first three worshipers to pick up an offering plate
get to be the deacons, and all the others sit down, knowing that
they have been out-hustled. Pennies, nickels, dimes, quarters,
and dollar bills were presented to the Lord by individuals who
make from 25 cents to 25 dollars a day in sheltered workshops,
supported employment settings, and independent competitive
employment sites. After the service, two people made it their
responsibility to put the money from the offering plates into
bags for the bank.

Marcus was ready to sing his solo when the last offering
plate was placed in the front of the chapel. Although he was
planning to sing with no accompaniment, he accepted my
invitation to provide an accordion background to his solo:
"Amazing grace! how sweet the sound, that saved a wretch like
me! I once was lost, but now am found, was blind, but now I
see." He sang with a rich baritone voice, very unlike the
monotone that I had come to experience in congregational
singing at the chapel. Marcus sang all four verses from memory. It was beautiful. When he had finished, the congregation of
believers at the chapel applauded to express their gratitude to
God for Marcus's gift to us that morning.

God's people at the chapel are indeed hungry for the Word
of God. But God's Word needs to be presented somewhat differently from a formal sermon or homily. The medium is as
much the message as the words to this body of Christians who
have a wide range of mental capabilities. The story of "Barnabas—the Encourager" was my Scripture lesson this morning.
I partially told, partially enacted, and partially read from the
book of Acts the story of one of the unique men of the early
church. I selected worshipers to be the apostle Paul, John

Mark, and Peter as I in the role of Barnabas interacted with and encouraged them. The "sermon" became a dialogue between myself and God's people. The energy level was high. Participation in the message was shared by almost everyone in the room. Then God's message became abundantly clear: "Because we are God's people, we need to develop our gift of encouraging one another."

As we parted by singing, "Praise God from whom all blessings flow . . . ," I thought to myself that the blessings of God were truly flowing today. For we were indeed "worshiping God in spirit and in truth." What a lesson in grace for me again today!

To Think About

1. What makes for a spirit-filled and a truth-filled worship experience?
2. Why can people in a setting like a chapel for handicapped persons have such vibrancy and genuineness in the sharing of their faith?
3. What can we learn from people with disabilities in our mutual worship of our God?
4. Why may a setting like a chapel not always be good for persons with disabilities?

Twenty

"I know how to paint God's grace, and I do it pretty well."

> *See, the* LORD *has chosen [Chris] . . . and he has filled [her] with the Spirit of God . . . to make artistic designs . . . and to engage in all kinds of artistic craftsmanship.*
>
> Exodus 35:30–33

Chris Lake is a gifted woman, gifted in the truest biblical sense of the word. I see her as having a creative gift from the Holy Spirit. She can't talk and she doesn't write stories. She doesn't walk and doesn't have full control of her arm movements. But she can paint! God's grace oozes out of a tube of paint and onto a canvas. But her gift of creative artistry is only one aspect of the many lessons of grace that she teaches us. Unless we get to know her as a child of God to whom God has given gifts and whom he is using, we might very well miss the many extraordinary ways by which God shares his grace through her.

Chris was born with cerebral palsy. The doctors and nurses did not at first pick up on the fact that she had this disability. However, her parents and the pediatrician soon realized that the stiffening of her body, the curvature of her spine, and other indicators pointed to a disability that would continue to cripple her for the rest of her life. As a child, she went through many corrective surgeries and spent long periods of time in the pediatric ward of Mary Free Bed Hospital. In those early years, so much of Chris's life was defined by what she could not do. Chris had cerebral palsy. Her spine was curved. Her bone structure was not the way it should be. The reality that she was not able to talk or walk or maintain her basic bodily functions defined her life. These disabilities were the first big barriers that she and those around her had to overcome. But focusing only on the negative, as they did at first, held her back from developing into the gifted woman she is emerging to be today.

In reality Chris was, and is, able to do and to be much more. By God's grace, a change in expectations has occurred for Chris and for others around her. The amazing history (history—God's story) of Chris is that God has blessed her with a grace-filled and joy-filled attitude and determination to overcome these barriers. Chris, her parents, and her friends have long ago stopped thinking about what Chris cannot do and started focusing on what she can do. God's power is indeed being made perfect in her weakness (see 2 Cor. 12:9).

Certainly her parents soon learned that Chris could communicate with them. It was a matter of how to read her unique ways of informing them what she was thinking of and feeling. Much like watching a mime doing a one-act play, they learned what Chris wanted by watching her facial expressions. Her face speaks volumes. Her excited smile is a message of agreement and affirmation; her poker face is her way of disagreeing or not wanting what is being presented to her. Her perplexed face is her way of questioning what is presented to her. Throughout her experiences as a child, Chris has communicated her feelings and intentions clearly. It became obvious that, though she had disabilities, Chris demonstrated the full intelligence to grasp what was going on around her and had the courage from God to hang on during very tough times.

Adaptive equipment unlocked doors in Chris's life. The expressive face was powerful, but it was not enough. One of the first adaptive tools that Chris was introduced to was a Bliss Board. A Bliss Board is like a lap tray that displays pictures of the activities, ideas, needs, and desires Chris might chose to communicate. Even though her arm movements are difficult to control, Chris was able to point to a picture of a bathroom to communicate her toiletry needs or to a picture of food when she was hungry and a glass of water when she was thirsty. The Bliss Board was eventually upgraded to a liberator. A liberator is modified computer in which Chris can point to pictures, type out words and sentences, and have these messages verbalized through a voice synthesizer within the liberator.

Chris showed her individuality when she picked out her synthesized voice for the liberator. She choose the voice of "Sexy Betty" to do her speaking for her. She continues to use the liberator to speak what is on her mind.

For a long time others pushed Chris around in a wheelchair. She was dependent on other people for her mobility. But she wanted more self-determination in her life, while at the same time she expressed doubts about whether she could handle this independence. The professionals working with her and her parents recognized her need to get a power wheelchair to enable her to go where she wants to. Recently, she took the controls of a three-speed power chair. She was tentative at first about using the controls. But she quickly learned how to go forward, to go right and left, and to back up with her machine. Her bewildered face sometimes gave her true emotions of fear and uncertainty away, but she has been determined to have control of her mobility. She soon moved from slow speed to medium and finally to fast speed. She spent hours in the parking lot and in the halls of the sheltered workshop where she spends most of her daytime hours during the week, learning how to back up, make turns, and maneuver around obstacles. Much like a teenager learning to drive an automobile, Chris took her power wheelchair training seriously and passed her "driving test" at the Rehabilitation Center with flying colors.

Perhaps Chris's life blossomed most when she was first introduced to her liberator several years ago. When she was asked what she would most like to do in her life, she typed out on the liberator and "Sexy Betty" announced to her work trainer, "I would like to paint." It was soon apparent that Chris knew what she wanted to do, and she insisted that she be given the opportunity to do it.

The work trainer and the occupational therapist at the center devised a headband that wrapped around Chris's head and firmly held a paintbrush. On the tray of her wheelchair, they placed containers of watercolors. In front of the tray was an easel holding a sheet of paper close enough to her that she could take the brush, dip it into the watercolors, and paint her picture. It was soon discovered that Chris has rapid movement of her eyes, making it difficult for her to focus her brush on her paper. She discovered a way to compensate for this difficulty and soon was placing the paints on her canvas exactly where she wanted them to be.

Those who saw her early pictures realized that Chris had talent as a artist, but her talent was in very raw form. Special efforts were made to get an art instructor from Kendall College of Art & Design; this instructor gave her art lessons and taught her the use of different art formats and the processes of getting her artwork in front of people. God's grace began to ooze out on canvas in increasingly improved work.

The first public display of her art was at a Disabilities Art Fair at Mary Free Bed, where she had spent weeks and months as a child. Her face beamed as she displayed her creative skills before the doctors and nurses who had grown to love her. She was using her God-given gifts, and she was proud of her accomplishment. Although her liberator was not at the art fair, it could easily have been programmed for "Sexy Betty" to say, "I know how to paint God's grace, and I do it pretty well."

Chris's art instructor taught her how to hold her own art shows, how to mat and frame her pictures, how to use canvas instead of paper for a base, and even how to make up business cards so that she could hand them out at art shows. In a matter of two or three years she has become known as a promising artist in the Grand Rapids community. Her art instructor realized Chris's potential and helped her connect with another artist and instructor who could develop her artistic talent even more. Her parents have stood behind her advancing career with a sense of pride and amazement. Chris began using oils and acrylics as the mediums of her artistic expression. She was outfitted with new and better headgear, which made her painting strokes more bold. Her selection of colors is unique to her paintings. More recently the art instructor has taught her to use her hand in making some paint strokes and to used colored markers.

As Chris continued to develop her "abilities" (the gifts of the Spirit that she has), the art community has taken note of this gifted person. In 1996 Chris Lake was commissioned by Mary Free Bed to do an art piece that was sold in limited editions. Chris determined that the proceeds would go to the Pediatric Unit of the hospital to give back to others what had been done for her.

She continues to do one-person art shows and enters her artwork in art competitions throughout the community. She has not stopped growing and developing. She has spoken before groups of high school, college, and seminary students.

She is exploring new art techniques. She is pleased that you can give praise to God for her gifts.

To Think About

1. How does looking at what a person can do rather than what she can't do assist in the development of God's gifts in that person?

2. Not all of God's people are artists, not all of God's people are evangelists, but all of God's people are gifted by the Holy Spirit. What gifts of the Spirit do you feel good about?

3. What do you think motivates Chris to keep going? What motivates you? Is there anything you can learn from Chris?

Twenty-One

"I want you to talk about that house with a lot of rooms."

In my Father's house are many rooms. . . . I am going there to prepare a place for you. . . . I will come back and take you to be with me. . . .

John 14:2–3

Frances lives in a big building with lots and lots of bedrooms. In fact, the building used to be a dormitory for nurses in training, but now has been converted into housing for persons with mental illnesses. However, today more people with Frances's disability are living in two- to six-bed homes or apartments with care attendants providing only limited care. But there still are a few of the dormitory-style living arrangements for people whom our society keeps at a distance. Usually they are a step up from the four-hundred-bed dormitory-style living in state institutions in which everyone shared huge rooms. Maybe for personal-care reasons, maybe for convenience reasons, but mostly for financial reasons Frances is one of a few people who still live in a house with forty individual bedrooms. Most of her friends are fellow residents who have a mental illness like hers. She truly lives in "a house with many rooms."

Frances did not always live in her forty-bedroom converted nurses' lodge. Until the age of eighteen she lived with her parents. Then she met the man of her dreams, was married, and had three children. Today that marriage is long over, but she still maintains periodic contact with her children. During the very early part of her marriage, her life began to change. She was given the diagnosis of paranoid schizophrenia as the chemistry of her brain changed and her sense of "the real world" also changed. It was not easy for her newlywed husband to cope with her mood swings and the constant suspicious nature that she displayed. Her children could not always depend on their mother to be there for them. As much as Frances wanted to be a good mother and a devoted wife, her mental illness made it hard for her to care for her family. She was sent to a state mental hospital at a time when lobotomies and shock treatment were the main forms of treatment for the "insane" or the "crazy"—dehumanizing names she sometimes remembers people calling her. Lithium, Prozac, Elleril, and other new medications have revolutionized her life in the past ten years.

Frances lives a fascinating life in a house with many bedrooms. She shares one bathroom with ten other women on her floor. Other men and women share similar arrangements on other floors. Together, forty men and women share large and small television lounges, a common dining room, and daily activities. Outings to the mall, to a restaurant, or to the Lake Michigan beach are the highlights of the week. For the most part, Frances does not let schizophrenia prevent her from sharing in most activities offered in her home. She loves to grow flowers and small plants in her small room. Pictures of kittens adorn the one place that she can truly call her home—her bedroom in the house with many rooms.

Frances loves her Catholic church. Sometimes when she does not feel like going to mass, she might attend the Christian Reformed Church down the street or the Baptist Church just a little farther down the street. But usually she is very willing to go to mass at her Catholic church when the opportunity arises. The denomination is not what matters to Frances. It is what Jesus has done by dying on the cross for her that matters. Christians getting together to worship by singing and praying and meditating—this is what counts to her. Bible studies with her friends, praying when someone is sick, visiting the sick—these are important. Saying her rosary daily is important. Frances is firm and very public about what she believes and practices. Tuesday Bible studies are some of the most treasured times for her because she can then sing her favorite songs: "The Old Rugged Cross," "Blessed Assurance, Jesus Is Mine," "Stand Up, Stand Up for Jesus," "Do Lord, Oh Do Remember Me." Frances sings them all from memory, and she sings them passionately.

Now in her late sixties, Frances has been having more medical problems. She has had reactions to some of the medications that have worked well for her, and several times these medical reactions have become near-death experiences. Even more significant has been the death of three or four of her friends—people who live with her in that house with many rooms. Recently one of her best friends died unexpectedly. One minute she was alive and well, and the next she was gone; and this traumatized Frances. For weeks she fixated on death—her friend's death, her own death, heaven, and hell—even purgatory, a belief of her Catholic tradition.

It was at this time that another of her friends, Sue, died of cancer. It was a staff decision to let Sue die "at home" in her bedroom with hospice care. We believed that it was important that the forty residents of the home face the issues of life and death, and though the experience would be hard for some people like Frances, we would be available to help them adjust to the death of one of our "family members." During the six or so weeks of Sue's rather rapid decline Frances visited her every day. Frances would sometimes pray with her and sometimes tell her how much she loved her and how much she would miss her when she died. Often we as a staff would learn that she would do little things that indicated that she really cared for Sue. Whenever our Bible study group met, Frances always reminded us to remember Sue in our prayers. Sometimes she would go out and pick flowers from a neighbor's flower garden and take them to Sue.

I received a hand-written note given to me by a home-care aide one Tuesday when I came in for the regular Bible study. It was from Frances: "Come to my room right after Bible study! Frances." Others told me that she had been in her room quite a lot lately, especially in the past two weeks. It dawned on me that it had been about two weeks since Sue died. So after the Bible study, I went to Frances's room.

As I knocked on the door, Frances called, "Come in, Reverend Al! Do you have your accordion? Bring your Bible! Get a piece of paper!" I happened to have my Bible and my accordion, which I had used for the Bible study group singing, but I needed to find a piece of paper. *What does she want?* I wondered.

Once I was inside, Frances started to talk nonstop as she sat up in her bed. "You know that 'house with many rooms' passage in the Bible?"

"You mean the passage in John 14 that says, 'Do not let your hearts be troubled. Trust in God; trust also in me. In my Father's house are many rooms; if it were not so, I would have told you. . . .'"

"Ya, that's the one, with many rooms. Well, I want you to read that Bible passage when I die. I have three daughters that I have not seen in years. I want you to find them and get them to my funeral. I want you to tell everyone here, and I want you to especially tell my daughters when I'm gone that I'm in that house with many rooms in heaven. Write it down on your paper! Tell 'em that Jesus took me there! And then I want you to take that accordion there and have everyone sing 'The Old Rugged Cross,' 'Blessed Assurance, Jesus Is Mine,' 'Stand Up, Stand Up for Jesus!' 'Do Lord, Oh Do Remember Me.' Write it all down on your paper! And don't forget to tell them that I am in that house with a lot of rooms! Write it all down on your paper so you won't forget!"

Obviously, Frances had been thinking very seriously about the important and eternal issues of her life. The death of friends and our own bouts with health issues that have life-and-death dimensions have a way of raising those questions for all of us. But they were clearly matters that she wanted be certain were taken care of before she died. As she talked, it struck me as ironic that she was already living and serving by faith in a "house of many rooms" on this earth. To look forward to a house of many rooms in eternity only seemed right. The hundreds of times Frances has come down to praise the Lord in our Bible study hour on Tuesdays, the many small gestures of Christian service to her friends in the old nurses' residence hall, the intense need to let her children know that she knew Jesus and she would be living in that house with many rooms in heaven, and the strong identity with God's people across the spectrum of the church community—all are part of her current life and ministry. I wonder if her ministry in heaven would look much as it is here on earth, only in a perfect way.

It is now about two years later. Frances has not died yet. She has had several scary times in the hospital when I thought that I might have to have her funeral—the one we planned and developed that Tuesday afternoon in her small room of the big house. I still have her "funeral paper." I am still reminded not to forget about that house with many rooms. And I am fully confident that Frances knows whose child she is and where she is going when God calls her home.

To Think About

1. Are you looking not only at your eternal home with God but also at the way those who know and love you see your eternal future?

2. What preparations have you made for your death and funeral?

3. How closely are you willing to live with the "living" and "dying" issues of your future and see them all as part of your life in Jesus Christ?

Twenty-Two

"I thank God for every new day."

> *Whatever you do, whether in word or deed, do it all in the name of the Lord Jesus, giving thanks to God the Father through him.*
>
> Colossians 3:17

God grant me the serenity to accept the things I cannot change, the courage to change the things I can, and the wisdom to know the difference." With these words another Alcoholics Anonymous meeting begins. The group-appointed leader for the meetings this month is Robert. "Hi, everyone. I'm Robert, and I am very grateful to God to be alive and sober at this meeting tonight." He really means it. He is welcomed by people who know him, who support him, and who have become some of his truest and dearest friends. "Hi, Robert," eighteen people in A.A. respond.

Robert says that he feels more accepted and loved in A.A. than in any other group of people, including his church. It bothers him that he makes this claim about the body of believers with whom he worships, but the reality is that the organized church has always kept him at arm's length. If the truth were told, he himself has also kept the church at a distance. Although Robert grew up in the church and his parents are committed Christians, he lived most of his childhood and adolescence doubting whether God exists and believing that church people are hypocrites.

So he acted up in Sunday school. He found excuses not to attend church activities. He avoided being associated with the church.

Like many other teenagers, he experimented with drugs and alcohol. He never felt that he was "hooked" on them, as he saw that some of his friends were who partied more than he. But he developed the capacity to drink a fifth of hard liquor in an evening without acting drunk. He never realized that this "tolerance to alcohol" was a clear signal that he was becoming addicted to it. On some occasions he didn't remember what happened for a period of time when he was drinking. These "blackouts" were also indicators of addiction to alcohol. His grandfather's drinking history could have suggested a genetic risk to alcoholism, but he would not have believed it if someone had explained the risk. Like his friends, he was drinking and "drugging" because "everyone does it," "it's cool to do it," and "it makes me feel so good." Not even his mother's harping at him for drinking made him take note of the danger he was facing.

Then one night after a high school basketball game, it happened. Robert started a fifth of whiskey just before the game. He thought no one noticed because he took his breath mints along with him. He drank more whiskey during the game as well. During several "bathroom breaks," he managed to finish the rest of what he had started before the game. And after the game, he opened another stash of beer that was under his car seat. Even though he ate the mints to cover the alcohol smell, most of his immediate friends recognized the smell and his increasingly loud and grandiose behavior in the stands. One of his drinking friends even commented to another drinking buddy that Robert had better not be driving after the game.

Well, Robert did drive that eventful evening. He fought off his other friends' insistence that he not drive, declaring that he was the best driver of the group. Unfortunately he was not the best driver when he was drunk. Only forty-five minutes after the basketball game, Robert and three of his friends failed to make a sharp turn on a country road and abruptly crashed into a tree. All of them had alcohol and pot in their bodies at toxic levels. Two of his friends died. One came out of the crash without a scratch. Robert went into a deep coma, having suffered a major traumatic head injury.

"I do thank God that I am his child, and I am alive and sober tonight," Robert tells the group when it is his turn to speak. "Let me tell you what it was like before, and what it is like now to have my God whom I have come to know and love as Jesus in my life. I want to tell you how I got here too. You see, it's only God's grace that allows me to tell you that I am celebrating my ten years of sobriety today. In three months and two days it will be fourteen years ago that I had my accident. But I began my sobriety ten years ago."

The group of eighteen recovering heroin, cocaine, and alcohol addicts explode with applause. In Alcoholics Anonymous, that applause is for God. Not everyone recognizes his or her "higher power" as the Triune God of Scripture—the Father and Creator of the Universe, the Son Jesus who is Savior and Lord, and the Holy Spirit who is the sustainer and encourager of our lives. But they do recognize that God gets them sober, God is with them when life is tough, and God as their Higher Power gets all the praise. Robert knows this too, but he believes this on a deeper level than most people. Since his accident, he has developed a real and dependent relationship with his God—Jesus Christ. And he is not afraid to tell this to others.

"I lived a pretty messed up life as an eighteen-year-old. I thought that I had my life in order, but really it was out of control. I did basically what I wanted to do just because I wanted to do it. My parents were totally frustrated with me. They could see how alcohol and drugs were destroying my life, but I couldn't. Then I had my accident. I don't remember much about the accident and the next two or three years after that. This is because of the brain damage I received in the crash. I learned from my parents that I was in a coma for three months. I couldn't lift my arms. I couldn't remember who I was at first. I had great difficulty walking. The guilt I felt for driving the car in which two of my best friends died was devastating. I kept looking for people who would sneak drugs and alcohol into my room at the Rehabilitation Hospital, but the staff prevented this from happening. When I had weekend passes from the hospital, I wanted a drink so bad I could taste it. In fact, I had my first "dry drunks" at that time. My folks told me that I acted like I was inebriated. I even felt as if I had hangovers when there was no way I could have had any alcohol or drugs. Those were miserable times because even then I did not accept the fact that I had a problem with alcohol or pot.

"It was when I was in the Transitional Living Program that the staff realized they needed to confront my addiction to alcohol. They didn't sense my problems with other drugs at that time. When they asked me if I would see a substance abuse counselor, I balked at the idea. I had God, and he saved me from my accident. There was nothing that God and I couldn't do, or so I thought. But I was actually bitter toward God. I hated the fact that I was not recovering from the accident quickly enough.

I had explosive outbursts of emotion at the staff, at my parents, and, when no one was around, even at God.

"The staff kept after me to see the substance abuse counselor; so to get them off my back I started counseling with him. And he told me that I had to go to Alcoholics Anonymous as well as receiving the counseling. That was ten years ago today. I fought going at first. Being with a bunch of drunks when I thought I wasn't one of 'those' people was hard for me to accept. But I heard the stories—stories that I could relate to—stories that were not exactly like mine, but I knew they were my story. In counseling, I found out about my drinking patterns, my craving for alcohol all the time, my family history with my grandpa, and my crummy attitude; all of these things suggested that I may have had an alcoholism problem. I did not want to believe my counselor at first. But at an A.A. meeting it all came together. I believe that at that meeting God convicted me that I did and always will have an addiction to alcohol. By his grace, I can stay sober—one day at a time. I eventually learned that if I continue to drink, I will continue to do damage to my brain.

"I learned so much about myself in that first year. A.A. meetings were my lifeblood in my attempt to stay sober. Speech and physical therapists addressed head-injury issues. The social worker helped my parents and me to work through problems between us that existed long before my accident. A psychiatrist discussed with me the medications I needed to take. The substance abuse counselor helped me realize that I was not only addicted to alcohol but also to pot and heroin. Today I am convinced that if I use any of these drugs, I will be back at the same place in my life that led to my accident. These professionals helped me to learn so much about myself. What's more important is that I have been changing. My attitude, my outlook on life, and my faith grew so much that first year. I am confident that my God was in the process.

"I still have memory problems, especially when it comes to things around my late teen and early twenty years. Sometimes I still want to give up. But I believe God has been putting people in my life—like you and like a few very close friends now in my church who are there for me, and I for them. I sponsor four people in A.A. who also have brain injuries. We who are addicted and have a head injury face problems that some of you will never experience. I am still growing. I still have to work on my relationships, especially with my church. I'm Robert. And I really do thank God today that I am alive and sober. Thank you."

"Thank you, Robert" is echoed by all the people at the meeting.

Because of my prior background as a chaplain in a Christian substance-abuse treatment center for ten years, I had the privilege of being Robert's counselor in the Transitional Living Center for persons with brain injury. This is his story with enough changes to protect his confidentiality and anonymity. Alcoholics Anonymous has been and continues to be the place where God is doing tremendous works of grace with chemically dependent persons. Robert has a dual diagnosis—chemical dependency and head injury, but many others in Alcoholics Anonymous, Narcotics Anonymous, and Cocaine Anonymous have only the chemical dependency "disability."

To Think About

1. What is the importance of "telling our stories" to others as a means of experiencing God's grace—both for ourselves and for those who hear us?

2. How do you approach people in ministry when they are turned off to the God-talk of "churchy" Christians but are spiritually starved for the Good News and the God of good news?

3. What lessons can you learn from Alcoholics Anonymous and other self-help groups that will make the life of your church truer to the Scripture's presentation of the gospel?

Twenty-Three

"Do *you* think I can do it? I need to know what *you* think."

> *Carry each other's burdens, and in this way you will fulfill the law of Christ. . . . for each of you should carry his own load.*
>
> Galatians 6:2, 5

As a thirty-six-year-old black man in a predominately white community, Harold can talk about a lifetime of memories of racial discrimination. But he will more readily tell of the painful incidents of discrimination he receives as a person with a major physical disability. His limited use of one arm and his pronounced limp are the result of a motorcycle accident that occurred five years ago. What really irritates him most is that when people look at him with his disability they discount his abilities and himself as a person. When others look at him, they seem to believe that he can't do anything. They feel they need to help him without ever asking him if he wants help. They feel sorry for him, or they pity him. He hates that. He hates it with a passion. He feels dehumanized, and he often gets angry about it.

Harold is not passive when he believes that others don't acknowledge him as a complete person. His "in your face" style of letting others know what he thinks and feels can be intimidating to people like me, who tend to be overly polite and cautious in our attempts to help.

When I first met Harold, his angry and abrupt words made it hard for me to really hear what he was saying about how others treat him. I quickly jumped to the conclusion that he was an angry black man with a chip on his shoulder. But I had to learn that his brusque, confrontational style of speaking was expressive of the culture in which he was raised, and what he had to say was yet another evidence of God's tough-love grace.

Over the past five years Harold has worked hard to overcome the results of the accident that has completely altered his life. He spent hours upon hours in the hospital physical therapy room as he was learning to walk again. His motivation for those long hours in rehabilitation came from a single painful memory of a doctor the night of his accident. The doctor in the hospital emergency room never realized that Harold overheard him tell a nurse that he believed Harold would never walk again. Harold has made it a personal goal to prove the doctor wrong. "Never say never" has been his motto. Ever so slowly, he put weight first on one leg and then on the other. Eventually, he learned to bear weight on both feet, but the strength in his right leg is much less than the strength in his left. He walks with a pronounced limp. But he walks. At one time he could not use his right arm at all; now with years of therapy he is able to lift his arm to the level of his face and use it to provide balance. He cannot grip anything with his right hand; however, he has developed extraordinary strength with his left arm and hand and does all the activities most of us need two hands to accomplish.

One of the reasons Harold arrived at Hope Network was to receive work training. This was the next phase of his rehabilitation process. So he was put in the work-training program to discover a whole new career. The area he was assigned to had many people who could function less than he. He very strongly felt that he was misplaced at first and verbalized this to people. He had served as a mechanic before his accident, and his first tasks at the sheltered workshop were to assemble plastic clothing hangers alongside persons with chronic disabilities. The assembly of the clothes hanger included putting together two clips on the connecting bar of the hanger. The clip assembly was a bit tricky for Harold because he had the use of only one hand in the assembly process. He almost walked off the job the first day when he saw Peter, who has Down's syndrome, quickly assemble hanger after hanger next to him. Whenever anyone noticed Harold's difficulty and tried to help him, he resisted with his in-your-face style of relating. It was *his* job, and he would find a way to do it.

He did find a way: he watched Peter assemble his hangers. Peter, who later became one of Harold's close friends, is not offended by his abrupt style. They are totally honest and straightforward with each other. What is more significant is the high level of acceptance each has with the other. Even though Harold's arm and leg are impaired, his mind is not. Harold soon devised a jig that would hold all the parts of his hanger together so that with one hand he could assemble his hangers as fast as or even faster than Peter. Over and over Harold demonstrated both creativity and mechanical ability at his job. It was soon apparent that he needed to move on to more complex tasks in his work training as he moved toward the day he would work again in competitive employment.

I have had contact with Harold many times during his work training. Our relationship was not always comfortable for me. But the breakthrough, not for him but for me, was the day he was put on a job that I thought might be too difficult for

him. He was working on a shrink-wrap machine that packaged
boat parts. As the chaplain of the organization, I often walk
around the work environments where people with disabilities
are doing their jobs. As I mill around, I pick up on what is
going on in the lives of others, and in this way I often discover
pastoral counseling needs. I call this ministry style a "ministry
of Christ's presence." It is focused more on being the "incarna-
tional Christ" with people than on doing something for them.

As I walked up to Harold, it became obvious to me that he
was having no difficulty putting the front red-and-green light
of a boat on the cardboard sheet with other lights. But when
the large cardboard sheet was to be placed in the shrink-wrap
machine, he found it difficult to move the sheet into the
machine with only one hand without spilling the whole sheet
of parts on the floor. Even though he was having difficulty, I
was the one who was frustrated.

Finally Harold noticed my frustration and responded to it.
"Well! Do *you* think I can do it? I need to know what *you*
think." I had thought Harold was so self-sufficient that he
didn't really care what others thought or expected of him. "You
might be surprised," he went on to say, "but I really do care
what others think about or expect from me. I might try to
prove them wrong. I might go way beyond what they or even
what I think I can do. But I really do want to know what *you*
think." The conversation was certainly not just about boat
lights on a piece of cardboard going into a shrink-wrap
machine. Harold soon mastered that job. But in our conversation he made his thoughts clear: Christians who care about
each other are there for each other. They speak their minds to
each other. They encourage each other. They know each other's
thoughts. They tell it like it is. They are not always going to
agree with each other, but they know where the other stands.

He added, "That's why Peter and I get along so well. He may not be very smart, and he may not always be right. But I know what he thinks and what he expects of me."

Harold really did care what the doctor in the emergency room thought. He really does want to know what I think he can do and be. Although Harold's blunt style of relationship might be a different cultural expression of caring than I am used to, it attempts to put into practice a value about Christian community with another person that I really believe is true. "Speaking the truth in love" (Eph. 4:15) is a way of "carry[ing] each other's burdens" (Gal. 6:2) while allowing each other to "carry his [or her] own load" (v. 5).

Having expectations about what one can do with one's life and knowing one's limitations are important realities for a person who has a disability. But those personal expectations of ourselves are always framed within the expectations and ideas that others have for us. Harold helped me learn yet another lesson of God's grace in the community of believers.

To Think About

1. How open are you to learning about God's grace from others whom you might otherwise keep at a distance because of relational style, personal disability, or cultural difference?
2. How do others' expectations and thoughts about you and your abilities influence you to become the person God wants you to be?
3. Think about and discuss the importance of an open and honest community of people around you who are willing to share their thoughts and expectations with you.
4. How are you personally encouraging others around you by sharing your hopes and desires for them and your expectations of them?

Twenty-Four

> "I don't know who Grace is, but I think God must love her a lot."

I became a servant of this gospel by the gift of God's grace given me through the working of his power.
Ephesians 3:7

Most school systems today are recognizing the importance of addressing the needs of students with different learning disabilities. In the Christian school system that my children have attended we have a Christian Learning Center, which helps students with a variety of learning, mental, and physical disabilities to complete their Christian education. This help has come in many forms: testing for learning disabilities, tutoring, personal-guidance counseling, consultation with teachers to help them adjust to the learning styles of the students, and support and guidance for the families of those with disabilities. This assistance has made it possible for many young people with disabilities to receive their education alongside their peers who may not have these difficulties. Inclusive education is the buzzword in most school systems. I am happy to see Christian schools provide inclusive education, not only for the needs of the children with disabilities, but also for all students who truly see how all of God's people are differently "abled."

Penny is receiving help from the same Christian Learning Center where one of my children was given assistance with his learning disability to enable him to complete his high school courses. She has Down's syndrome and functions at a comparatively high level. Today she is a sophomore in high school. She has been in "inclusive education" for all of her educational career. Certainly she is not an *A* student nor will she ever be, but with the help she receives from a tutor and with the assistance her teachers get from an educational specialist, Penny is able to have the same Christian education that her parents want for all three of their children.

Maybe because Penny has a most pleasant and outgoing personality, maybe because she and her schoolmates realize quite naturally that she is not really so very different from the rest of her friends, and maybe because many people behind the scenes are making the "inclusive educational process" work, Penny is doing better than most other students in high school. She is passing her classes. She has a positive outlook in her life. Her peer relationships are especially healthy. Of course, sometimes she wishes that she would be asked out on a date, as some of her friends are. She is absolutely convinced that every sophomore in high school dates and that only she does not. She doesn't realize that actually not many sophomores date, and that most, like her, wish they did. She is invited to the same activities that her friends attend. She won a spot on the cheerleading squad, but she often comes late to practice because of her afternoon class time with her tutor. All in all, Penny is a normal teenager, living and working like her fifteen- and sixteen-year-old colleagues.

She is also an active member of her church youth group. Her involvement with the teens at church is much like her involvement with her peers at school. Her loving, effervescent personality rubs off on her friends. She sparks much of the energy that flows in church education classes and in her church youth program. Some of the words and ideas that she shares with others reveal that she doesn't have a total grasp of the issue being talked about, but her Christian character shines through so strongly that others accept her anyway.

Penny's genuine and sterling Christian character radiated in a youth group meeting one Sunday evening. The young people were discussing the topic "The Importance of Belonging." Some topics grab young people, and they run with it; some topics do not. This one did. The conversation was lively. One of the guys told of an incident when he was not included in a skiing outing to which he had been sure the group would invite him. He felt hurt and angry when the others took off and left him home. He believed at first that the group had done it intentionally. Later he learned that two people in the group had thought the other had called to invite him. On the way up to the ski lodge, they discovered that neither of them had made the call, and the whole group had a rather gloomy Saturday on the ski slopes because their friend was not along.

Penny and the other church youth group members easily identified with the young man. Some chimed in with stories of their own. But one of the young women in the group expressed an insight that held the promise of new wisdom. "I wonder," she said, "I wonder, if the real issue behind belonging is knowing and feeling that we are accepted—I mean totally accepted by our friends—and maybe, ultimately, being totally accepted by God and really knowing it." That created a real buzz of conversation, with several people talking at once. One person started to speak about how horrible it is to feel rejected, another told what being accepted meant to her, and a third talked about many practical ways in which we experience "grace."

Penny didn't really pick up on everyone's words because they were all speaking at the same time, but she did hear the word "grace." The others all stopped when they realized that everyone was talking at the same time and that no one had the attention of the whole group. After absolute silence for half a second the entire youth group heard Penny brilliantly declare, "I don't know who Grace is, but I think God must love her a lot." Her words brought the house down. But they were words that reflected clearly who Penny is and what her life meant to the others in the group.

True, she might not know how to define or even describe "grace," but Penny's life radiates God's "unconditional love" to all those around her. And her love for others reflects God's unconditional love for her.

I believe that the story of Penny reflects the stories of the many others about whom I have written in this book. God's people who experience disabilities may, or in many cases may not, understand how to define or describe God's grace. They may or they may not know that they truly are ambassadors of that grace. But they live it. Their stories are contemporary parables of God's grace to teach God's body of believers what it means to live in his kingdom. It is my prayer that reading *Parables of Hope* may have inspired you in your Christian life. But more than that, I pray that you may reach out to your Christian brothers and sisters who are differently abled and include them in the one unified and caring "body of Jesus Christ."

To Think About

1. What has been your experience in learning about God's grace from his people with disabilities?

2. What initiative are you going to take to get to know the "Graces" whom God loves "a lot" and who with that love can love you a lot?

3. What impact do you expect this book to have on your Christian life?

4. What differences will it make in your relationships to others?